Series / Number 07-061

MULTIPLE COMPARISONS

ALAN J. KLOCKARS
GILBERT SAX
University of Washington

SAGE PUBLICATIONS
The International Professional Publishers
Newbury Park London New Delhi

Printed in the United States of America

For information address:

SAGE Publications, Inc.
2455 Teller Road
Newbury Park, California 91320

SAGE Publications Ltd.
6 Bonhill Street
London EC2A 4PU
United Kingdom

SAGE Publications India Pvt. Ltd.
M-32 Market
Greater Kailash I
New Delhi 110 048 India

International Standard Book Number 0-8039-2051-2

Library of Congress Catalog Card No. 86-61912

97 98 99 10 9 8

When citing a university paper, please use the proper form. Remember to cite the correct Sage University Paper series title and include the paper number. One of the following formats can be adapted (depending on the style manual used):

(1) IVERSEN, GUDMUND R. and NORPOTH, HELMUT (1976) "Analysis of Variance." Sage University Paper series on Quantitative Applications in the Social Sciences, 07-001. Beverly Hills: Sage Pubns.

OR

(2) Iversen, Gudmund R. and Norpoth, Helmut. 1976. *Analysis of Variance.* Sage University Paper series on Quantitative Applications in the Social Sciences, series no. 07-001. Beverly Hills: Sage Pubns.

CONTENTS

Series Editor's Introduction

The very first volume in this series, Iversen and Norpoth's *Analysis of Variance*, has indicated by its sales that the topic is of interest to a wide audience. But as useful as ANOVA is, it stops after asking whether differences exist among groups. Often, however, there are multiple levels of the independent variable, and these kinds of designs are only partially analyzed with the decision that group differences exist. Additional questions remain about where, within levels of the independent or "treatment" variable, the differences are accounted.

Multiple Comparisons by Alan J. Klockars and Gilbert Sax describes the most important methods used to investigate differences between levels of an independent variable within an experimental design. Starting with a review of the analysis of variance and hypothesis testing, the authors describe the dimensions on which multiple comparisons vary. Chapters 2, 3, and 4 describe methods in which (a) the basic questions are determined before data are collected, (b) there are post hoc comparisons involving pairs of means, and (c) there are post hoc comparisons of combinations of groups. Chapter 5 applies the methods described in earlier chapters to factorial designs with particular attention to testing comparisons of interaction. The last chapter is concerned with issues regarding sample size and violations of assumptions.

Throughout the monograph Klockars and Sax make use of a single example based on a famous experiment by Solomon Asch on group conformity. Using the same treatment groups, the authors show how each multiple comparison method would be appropriate—depending on the information the researchers sought from the experiment.

A virtue of the work is that the authors present alternative methods that could be used to answer the same experimental question. In most instances the choice is one of a tradeoff between better safeguards against incorrectly identifying differences as significant and an enhanced ability to detect true experimental differences. Therefore the monograph describes the statistical power of each method discussed.

The volume provides the reader with an introduction to the most commonly used and most important multiple comparison tests along with a thorough description of how these tests are similar and how they differ from one another. With this information the reader will not only know how to conduct multiple comparisons in experimental designs but should also be better able to understand and evaluate published research. In addition, readers will be pleased at the care with which the volume is written and with the clever use of the one, extended sample.

—*Richard G. Niemi*
Series Co-Editor

MULTIPLE COMPARISONS

ALAN J. KLOCKARS
GILBERT SAX
University of Washington

1. MULTIPLE COMPARISONS

Social science research is conducted frequently to compare the effects of two experimental conditions. Educators may be concerned with the presence or absence of *advance organizers* (formal cues providing a scheme for a text passage); sociologists may be concerned with families in which both parents or only one parent is present; and economists may be interested in differences between third world and more affluent societies. Although there are many difficult aspects involved in any of these studies, the comparison of interest can be conceptualized easily since there are only two levels of the experimental variable being compared. If a difference exists, it is an easy matter to compare the means to determine which of the two levels is higher.

Although the two-level design meets the needs of some researchers, many others have to consider independent variables that are more complex. The educator may be interested in different kinds of advance organizers (e.g., chapter introductions in prose, the use of opening questions, lists of important ideas) and may wish to investigate whether these "organizers" should be placed at the beginning of a chapter, at crucial points within the chapter, or even as a chapter summary. Similarly, families exist in many differing configurations other than both parents present or one absent (absence, for example, can be due to death, disappearance, divorce, etc.). For the economist and political scientist, differences among specific continents or countries may be of greater interest than differences between third world and economically more advanced countries. When independent variables increase in complexity beyond two levels, uncertainty is created concerning the specific locations of any differences. To know that the estimated per capita income differs for five continents does not tell the investigator which of these continents are different from the others. The finding of significant differences among the five levels of the independent variable only represents a first step in describing the data. A second step involves the examination of the data to locate just which continents differ from the others. The purpose of this monograph is to describe the methods used to compare differences among three or more levels of the independent variable.

Multiple comparisons differ on two major dimensions: first, they ask different kinds of questions about the specific relationships among the levels of the independent variable. Some investigators are interested in exploring the differences observed among the treatments to discover whatever relationships might exist between them, while other investigators have a few a priori hypotheses that will be tested by the data. Second, within the methods designed to answer the same question, one can find different concerns for the relative likelihood of a decision error. We will consider both of these topics in later chapters.

The multiple comparison procedures described in this monograph are developed within the framework of an analysis of variance. This reflects the historical origins of the methods. The underlying principles, however, are equally applicable to other statistical procedures designed for research methods other than those involving experiments. The major principle common to all methods is the generation of meaningful specific questions to be investigated and the determination of proper control over decision errors.

The study of multiple comparisons is one of the most vital and controversial within statistics. This monograph will describe the more commonly used methods. The material covered should provide the information needed to conduct traditional multiple comparisons in most situations and the background to read more advanced works in professional and academic journals.

THE EXAMPLE

The primary example used throughout the monograph is based on a procedure developed by Solomon Asch (1951) to study group conformity. In his procedure male subjects were recruited for a visual discrimination experiment. The task was to observe three lines and to select the line having the same length as the standard line that was also presented. The subject was part of a group of seven men who were participating simultaneously in the experiment. The subject was seated in the sixth position around a table. The experiment seemed mundane and simple for the first few trials. Because of the small number of subjects, the experimenter suggested that, in succession, each person tell him which line was equal in length to a standard line. The early examples were easy, and all subjects agreed on the correct line. On the third trial, however, the subject is suddenly made aware that his estimate differs from the unanimous but incorrect judgments of the other participants in the experiment. The subjects are choosing one of the lines that is quite different in length from the standard line. The question is what the subject's response will be when faced with the unanimously incorrect responses of the other subjects.

Unknown to the experimental subject, Asch had recruited six of the participants to act as his confederates. On 12 trials the confederates provided unanimous but incorrect answers, and the score received by the subject was the number of times he gave the conforming (and incorrect) answer. Although there was considerable variability in the amount of conformity in different subjects who participated in the procedure, the average yielding to the group norm amounted to about 35% of the total judgments made. Evidently, the need to conform to group judgments is strong despite the fact that (1) there was no penalty for responding correctly, and (2) there was no apparent reward for agreeing with the obviously wrong but unanimous judgments of the other raters.

Following this early work, Asch and others (Asch, 1952, 1956; Crutchfield, 1959; Gerard, Wilhelmy and Connolley, 1968) continued the study of conditions that affect conformity within groups. For a review of the research, the interested reader is referred to Allen (1965).

The multiple comparison procedures described in this monograph will be illustrated with an example based on a combination of findings from the conformity studies. Although the data are fictitious and designed specifically to illustrate some of the concepts in multiple comparison testing, they have been constructed to reflect the actual experimental findings.

In Chapters 2, 3, and 4, the same five treatment groups described below will be used to show planned comparisons, pairwise comparisons, and Scheffé's Test. The primary consideration in these chapters is to demonstrate how the experimental question of interest differs for the various techniques and to demonstrate their importance and usefulness.

The basic design will be modeled closely after the original Asch paradigm. Each subject is run separately in the presence of either 3 or 6 confederates of the experimenter who determines their responses. A randomized group design is used in which 25 subjects will be assigned randomly to each of five treatment conditions. For each subject there will be 12 critical trials (out of a total of 30 trials) on which some or all of the confederates provide choices that are obviously incorrect. The dependent measure is the number of conforming responses made by the subjects. The treatment groups are described as follows:

I. Group I consists of 6 confederates and the subject who is seated in the sixth position. On the first two trials, all subjects will respond correctly. On the third trial and on a total of 12 trials, the 6 confederates are to give the same but incorrect response.

II. Group II is similar to Group I except that it consists of only 3 confederates; the subject is seated in the last position.

III. Group III is similar to Group I in size and in the location of the subject. It differs in that the person in position 2 differs from the other confederates by giving the correct response on all 12 critical trials.

IV. Group IV is similar to Group III in size and in subject location; one confederate also breaks from the other confederates on the 12 critical trials. It differs from Group III in that the person in position 2 responds with another incorrect response on the critical trials that differs from the responses of the majority of confederates.

V. Group V is similar to Group I in size and in location of the actual subject. On the critical trials, all 6 confederates provide the same, incorrect response. It differs from Group I in that on 10 of the noncritical trials (including trials 1 and 2), the person in the second position is the only confederate to give an incorrect response.

The first treatment represents the approach originally used by Asch. Theoretically, the need to conform should be strongest within this group. The remaining 4 groups all contain elements that are designed to reduce the need for conforming. Treatment II, for example, is smaller, while Treatments III, IV, and V contain some reduction in the unanimity of the group. The means of the 5 treatment groups are presented in Table 1.

The first question of interest in the experiment is whether all sample means are estimates of a common underlying population mean. If so, there is no additional analysis required since there would be no differences to explore. If, however, the 5 means cannot be assumed to come from a single population, we are forced to explore the ways in which the 5 groups differ from one another. To provide a common

TABLE 1
Means Number of Conforming Responses

	Group Description	$\bar{X}$
I.	7 members (unanimous on critical trials)	5.20
II.	4 members (unanimous on critical trials)	5.08
III.	7 members (one subject correct on critical trials)	2.44
IV.	7 members (one subject deviant on critical trials)	3.76
V.	7 members (one subject deviant on noncritical trials)	3.44

background and starting point, we will begin with a review of the analysis of variance (ANOVA).[1]

THE NULL HYPOTHESIS

The procedures for carrying out an ANOVA require that the researcher initially hypothesize that all treatments had equal effects. This statement of equality in the underlying parameters is called the *null hypothesis* because it asserts no treatment differences in the populations. In our example the null hypothesis (symbolized by *Ho*) is that the 5 configurations of group conformity had the same effect on the underlying populations. Although researchers rarely believe that Ho is true, the strategy calls for treatment differences that are large enough to reject Ho as being tenable. If the hypothesis is rejected that the treatments produced the same effect, the conclusion must be that some treatments produced different effects. The rejection of Ho would indicate that at least two different effects were produced by the treatments. Because Ho is always a statement regarding populations (the sample means are *estimates* of these population values), the rejection of Ho indicates our belief that the sample means are estimates of at least two *different* population means.

VARIANCE ESTIMATES OR MEAN SQUARES

The decision to reject or not to reject the Ho is based on a comparison of two mean squares. A mean square (MS) is an average of squared deviations. It is found by first summing the squared deviations (called the *sum of squares*) and then dividing by a function of the number of deviations involved, which is referred to as the number of *degrees of freedom* or *df*.

The *between-groups* mean square is based on the deviations of the treatment means from the grand mean. Because there is a direct relationship between the amount the scores vary and how much sample means based on those scores will vary, the differences between the treatment means from the grand mean can be used to generate an estimate of the variability in scores. Because this mean square is defined by the variability in the treatment means, its degrees of freedom are a function of the number of treatment groups or, more specifically, k–1.

The *within-groups* mean square is based on the differences of the scores within a treatment from the treatment mean. Each treatment group provides a separate estimate of the within-groups variability. Assuming *n* subjects in each sample, each treatment group's estimate is based on n–1 degrees of freedom. In most applications of the analysis of variance, these separate estimates are averaged or pooled to provide one stable estimate of the within-groups MS. This "pooling" is accomplished by summing all of the squared deviations from each treatment group to form the *within-groups sum of squares*. To obtain the *mean square within groups*, this sum of squares is then divided by the *within-groups degrees of freedom*. The degrees of freedom within-groups is found by adding the number of degrees of freedom within each group. With equal numbers of cases within each group, the within-groups degrees of freedom is k(n–1).

The conformity experiment contains 5 treatment groups. The between-groups MS will have k–1 or 4 degrees of freedom. Each treatment group has 25 subjects; thus the random differences between individuals within a group would have 25–1 degrees of freedom. Pooling each of the 5 estimates provides a within-groups estimate based on 5(25–1) = 120 degrees of freedom.

The magnitude of the mean square between groups (MS_b) depends on whether Ho is true or false. If Ho is true, the MS_b will provide an estimate of the *random variability* of the scores; if false, there are differences in the treatment means that reflect differential treatment effects. The variability among the sample means would be greater than would be expected solely because of random influences. As treatment groups show greater differential effects and as sample sizes increase, the MS_b will be increased. If Ho is true (i.e., no differences are found between the population means), the MS_w and the MS_b will both estimate the random variances of scores in the population. Thus the two values should approximate each other. However, if Ho is not true (i.e., the population means are not equal), then MS_b should be larger than the MS_w.

THE F-RATIO

In a randomized groups analysis of variance the F-ratio[2] is found by dividing the MS_b by the MS_w. As noted in the preceding paragraph, the MS_b and the MS_w will both estimate random variability if Ho is true. The distribution of MS_b/MS_w will be a right-skewed distribution about unity when Ho is true; when Ho is false, the ratio will increase since the variability between groups will be larger than the variability within groups. The F-ratio, like other statistics, has a sampling distribution that permits us to determine the probability that a particular value of *F* will be observed if Ho is true. When the probability is small that an F-ratio as large as or larger than the observed value will be found in the F-distribution, the experimenter might conclude that the F-distribution does not, in fact, describe the observed ratio. Because the F-distribution describes what will happen when Ho is true, rejecting the observed F-ratio as one that is derived from the F-distribution also rejects Ho as being true.

The random differences in the variance estimates determine the extent to which the F-ratios will vary when Ho is true. In turn, this depends on the number of degrees of freedom each variance in the ratio has. A different F-distribution exists for each pairing of degrees of freedom for the numerator (which is associated with the MS_b) and the denominator (which is associated with the MS_w). In general, these ratios are more closely distributed about unity as the df for either mean square increases. Virtually all statistics books contain tables indicating the F-values that set off the largest 5% and 1% of the ratios.

DECISION RULES AND STATISTICAL SIGNIFICANCE

The analysis of variance summary table for the conformity experiment can be found in Table 2. The observed value of *F* is 6.39, with df = 4

TABLE 2
Analysis of Variance Summary Table for Group Conformity Experiment

Source of Variability	*Sum of Squares*	*df*	*Mean Square*	*F*
Between groups	135.25	4	33.81	6.39*
Within groups	634.80	120	5.29	
Total	770.05	124		

*p < .05.

in the numerator of the F-ratio and df = 120 in the denominator. The question is whether the observed value of F is consistent with Ho, or whether the ratio is too large to believe that Ho is true. Although very large F-ratios can occur by chance, it is very unlikely that they will do so. At some point—however arbitrary that point may be—the experimenter must state that Ho will be rejected. By custom and by acquiescence, the .05 level is the usual critical probability of incorrectly rejecting Ho (in some experiments this probability may be decreased to .01). As noted previously, this probability—.05 or .01—is known as *the level of significance* and is denoted by an alpha. With alpha set at .05 and with 4 and 120 degrees of freedom, the critical value of F needed to reject Ho is 2.44. The *decision rule* that states the conditions for rejecting or failing to reject Ho is that the experimenter will not reject Ho if the F-ratio can be counted among the lower 95% of those ratios that occur by chance (i.e., when Ho is true) and to reject Ho if the F-ratio is among the largest 5% that occur with a true Ho. Since the largest 5% of F-ratios begin at 2.44 for 4 and 120 dfs, the observed value of $F = 6.39$ is among those largest F-values that might occur by chance. Thus we reject Ho at the .05 level and conclude that at least two different effects were produced by the 5 treatments. As noted previously, the purpose of this monograph is to describe methods to determine which treatments account for the rejection of Ho.

DECISION ERRORS

The probability always exists that an experimenter may reject Ho when, in fact, Ho is true. Declaring that a significant difference exists when it does not is known as a *Type I error*; the reciprocal error of failing to find a significant difference when there is one is known as a *Type II error*. In the conformity experiment, F-ratios larger than 2.44 will occur by chance 5% of the time. Because the computed value of the F-ratio was 6.39, we would reject Ho and conclude that the 5 treatment means do not act as if they were all drawn at random from the same population. However, the possibility exists that our results reflect the operation of a Type I error since our F-ratio might be included among the largest 5% of those ratios that occurred by chance. Because the significance level chosen by the experimenter determines the probability of committing a Type I error, these errors could be reduced by lowering the alpha region from .05 to .01. The penalty for doing so, however, is an increase in Type II errors.

Type II errors are influenced by many factors but especially by the magnitude of the treatment effects. If treatment effects are large, they are more easily detected by tests of significance. Another factor that influences Type II error is random variability. When random variability is large, it is difficult to detect true differences since sample means would be expected to vary considerably by chance, and real differences among the groups would be obscured. Type II errors are also affected by sample size. The larger the sample sizes are on which the means are based, the more readily will the differences be detected. The *power*[3] of a statistical test is determined by its ability to avoid Type II errors by correctly rejecting Ho. We will discuss the power of each multiple-comparison test in the remaining chapters.

SELECTING THE MOST APPROPRIATE MULTIPLE-COMPARISON TEST

The choice of a multiple-comparison test depends primarily on the experimental questions to be answered. Sometimes the experimenter needs to compare each mean with each of the other means. With 5 sample means there are 10 separate pairs of means to be tested against one another. But other experiments may require the researcher to compare one group mean against the combined mean of some or all remaining means. Other complex configurations of means might also need to be analyzed for significance. Knowing which questions are relevant to an experiment determines, in part, which multiple comparison test should be selected.

Knowing the questions to be asked, however, does not complete the researcher's task. Usually several procedures are available that could provide answers to the same experimental question. These procedures differ in the degree of control they exercise over Type I errors (i.e., the erroneous rejection of a true Ho) for a specific comparison. These methods differ from one another by specifying how large a difference must be before it is declared significant. Thus it is possible for experimenters to reach different conclusions regarding the rejection of a specific Ho depending on the method chosen for analyzing the data.

SELECTING A MULTIPLE-COMPARISON TEST AND TYPE I ERRORS

As noted previously, the erroneous rejection of Ho is called a Type I error. In testing many different comparisons, the chance of committing a Type I error increases (unless the error is specifically controlled) because there are numerous decisions made within a single experiment. Although multiple comparison tests purport to control Type I errors to 5%, the meaning of that value differs depending on the particular method selected. In some procedures, for example, the 5% refers to the chance that a *single* decision will falsely reject Ho; for others, it is the chance that an error will occur *anywhere* within the set of possible decisions. The disparities in definitions of a Type I error and the varieties of experimental questions that could be addressed lead to different multiple-comparison tests presented in this paper.

DEFINITIONS AND MEANINGS OF TYPE I ERRORS IN MULTIPLE-COMPARISON TESTS

If an experiment involves a single decision (as does the t-test or an overall ANOVA), the probability of committing a Type I error, assuming Ho is true, is the chance that the data will result in rejection of that hypothesis. Multiple comparisons, however, involve multiple decisions. As a result, there are several ways to describe the Type I error rate.

ERROR RATE PER COMPARISON

The error rate per comparison is the probability that a Type I error will occur on a single comparison. It is analogous to the definition of Type I error for the overall test of significance. Assuming a 5% significance level, 5% of the comparisons (in a series of independent comparisons where Ho is true) would result in a rejected null hypothesis. The important point is that the recurring sampling element is the comparison itself. The 5% refers to a percentage of comparisons that would be expected to be significant by chance over many such independent comparisons.

ERROR RATE EXPERIMENTWISE OR FAMILYWISE

Instead of the comparison being the sampling unit, the error rate experimentwise depends on the experiment itself as the sampling unit. A 5% error rate experimentwise means that 5% of the experiments would be expected to contain one or more comparisons that would result in a Type I error, assuming that the complete Ho for the experiment is true and that the experiment is repeated many times. The error rate experimentwise describes the probability that an experiment involving several comparisons will result in a Type I error on one or more of these comparisons.

An alternative definition of the experimentwise error rate is that it is the probability of incorrectly rejecting one or more true null hypotheses given either a true *complete null hypothesis* or *partial null hypotheses*. A true partial Ho means that some, but not all, of the treatment conditions are drawn from the same population. In the example the complete Ho is that all treatments have the same effect. A partial Ho is that some subset of the means produced equal effects. For example, if the true treatment effects were that the two unanimous groups produced identical results whereas a different but equal effect was produced by the remaining groups, there would be two partial null hypotheses that would be true. The likelihood of an experimentwise error would be the probability that either of these partial null hypotheses would be rejected. This alternative definition will be referred to as *the worst case experimentwise error rate* because a number of true partial null hypotheses represents the greatest threat of a Type I error.

ERROR RATE PER EXPERIMENT

The error rate per experiment is the *number* of Type I errors that occur in an experiment involving several comparisons. The error rate per comparison and the error rate experimentwise are *probabilities* with minimum and maximum values of 0.00 and 1.00, respectively; the error rate per experiment is a *count* of errors that has no theoretical upper limit except, of course, for the number of comparisons made.

TYPES OF MULTIPLE COMPARISONS

Most multiple comparisons can be categorized as being (1) a limited number of comparisons arising from the statement of a priori hypotheses; (2) comparisons of all or a fewer number of pairs of means; and (3) exploratory analyses of combinations of groups as well as of pairs of means. Each type of multiple comparisons will be described in greater detail.

LIMITED NUMBER OF COMPARISONS BASED ON A PRIORI HYPOTHESES

In many studies the experimenter is able to specify the research hypotheses so that they may be answered by a few, planned comparisons. The nature of these comparisons may vary from simple comparisons of two means to more complex analyses involving trends or differential weighting of groups. Sometimes the set of proposed comparisons will be independent of or *orthogonal* to one another, while other comparisons will be redundant or nonorthogonal.

One advantage of limiting the number of comparisons is that Type I errors are less likely to accumulate since there are fewer opportunities for them to be generated. Planned comparisons are also advantageous since the experimenter is unable to capitalize knowingly on specific chance differences within the set of means. Among those tests that are usually placed within this category are *orthogonal* and *polynomial* comparisons, *nonorthogonal* comparisons, and *Dunn's test*. These tests are described in Chapter 2.

PAIRWISE COMPARISONS OF MEANS

A common procedure used to explore differences in treatment means is to compare all possible pairs of means. In pairwise comparisons the treatment groups are not combined but are treated individually. The number of comparisons possible within a set of *k* treatment groups is $k(k-1)/2$. Thus, for the study on group conformity there could be as many as 10 separate pairs of means to be compared. The decisions would be whether there was a difference in the effectiveness of each pair of treatments. As the number of groups increases, the number of comparisons increases rapidly.

The methods used to analyze pairwise comparisons (to be described in greater detail in Chapter 3) include the Least Significant Difference test as well as methods proposed by Tukey, Duncan, and Newman-Keuls.

EXPLORATORY ANALYSIS

In some exploratory research studies the experimenter may be unwilling or unable to restrict the number of comparisons to a few limited hypotheses. Instead, the intent of the study may be to search for whatever relationships may be present in the data. The experimenter might search to detect pairwise differences as well as differences among sets of means. If treatment groups contain no obvious common elements, the analysis will usually consist of all pairwise comparisons; if there are common and interpretable elements, the experimenter may want to test those combinations that appear to represent meaningful differences by using the Scheffé Test (see Chapter 4).

In exploratory studies the experimenter is usually unaware of the number of hypotheses that eventually will be investigated. Because these hypotheses are suggested by examining the data obtained in the course of the study, the researcher might unknowingly be capitalizing on chance occurrences that lead to Type I errors.

TEST STATISTICS

Multiple-comparison procedures differ in the test statistic generated to evaluate statistical significance. Pairwise comparisons usually involve the q statistic while planned comparisons and exploratory analyses use the t- or F-ratios.

THE t-TEST

The t-test is the classical conceptualization of a significance test on the difference between two means. The t-test divides the difference between means by the standard error of the difference between the means. This form has been adopted in several multiple-comparison procedures to produce a test statistic.

The denominator of the t-test is the standard error of the difference between means. This standard error is a function of the variability of observations and the sample size. In this application the best estimate of the random variability of observations is usually the mean square that was used in the denominator of the test for the overall treatment effects. In the randomized group design this is the within-groups mean square. In Chapter 6 we will describe other approaches to use when the within-groups mean square is inappropriate. The sample sizes for the standard error of the difference between means are the actual number of subjects on which each mean was computed.

THE q-STATISTIC

The q-statistic is commonly used in pairwise comparisons. Like the t-statistic, q is a measure of distance expressed in standard error units. The q differs from t in that it uses the *standard error of the mean* as the denominator rather than the *standard error of the difference between means*. The difference in the denominators is dictated by a different perspective on the question of interest. When the t-statistic is used, the random variable is the *difference between two means*. If Ho were true, this variable would have a mean of zero and a standard error that would describe the variability of *differences between means*. The q-statistic, however, is based on the variability of *sample means*. The test evaluates the likelihood that the largest and smallest means in a group of k means were drawn from the same population—that is, that the means were selected from a common sampling distribution. Tables are available that describe the number of standard errors that two means can be apart and still be considered to be drawn from the same sampling distribution. These tables take into account the desired level of significance, the number of treatment groups being compared, and the number of degrees of freedom on which the standard error depends.

Although q is used to determine whether the two most extreme means differ significantly, it may also be used to test the homogeneity of all intermediate means. If the two extreme means are declared to be drawn from the same population, all intermediate sample means are also considered to be derived from that population.

THE F-STATISTIC

Procedures involving an F-ratio constitute a third statistic used in multiple comparisons. The information provided by an F-ratio with one degree of freedom (df) in the numerator is equivalent to that provided by a two-tailed t-test. The numerical value of the F-ratio will equal t^2 for that comparison. Although they provide equivalent information, the computation of the two statistics differs and requires elaboration.

The F-statistic is the ratio between two mean squares. The numerator of this ratio is a mean square involving the comparison of interest between the means, and the denominator is a measure of random variability. If Ho were true for a particular comparison, the numerator and denominator would both estimate a common population variance; if false, the variability found in the numerator would be greater than the variability in the denominator.

An easy algorithm for calculating the mean square for the comparison of interest starts by constructing a linear combination of treatment means. Each treatment group's mean is multiplied by a weight which is so selected that the sum of the products will have an expected value of zero if Ho is true and be different from zero if Ho is false. The configuration of the weights reflects the comparison being investigated. For example, the conformity experiment has 5 treatment groups. One comparison of interest might be whether the mean for the larger unanimous group (Group I) differs significantly from the mean for the smaller unanimous group (Group II) with no consideration given to the remaining groups. If the two groups of interest are, in fact, estimates of the same population mean, the sum produced by multiplying the means by the vector of weights (1, –1, 0, 0, 0)[4] would have an expected value of zero. However, if the first group produces greater conformity than the second, the sum of the products will be positive since the first group is multiplied by a +1 and the second group by a –1.

More complex weights are used for more complex comparisons. For example, a comparison of interest might be the difference between the average of the first two groups with the average of the remaining three. The weights to address this question are 3, 3, –2, –2, –2. Note that the weights always sum to zero, so that if Ho were true and the population means were equal, the sum of the products would differ from zero only by an amount produced by the random differences in the estimates of the means.

The sum of the products of the weights and the means is referred to as *D*, as shown in equation 1.1:

$$D = (a\overline{X}_1 + a\overline{X}_2 \ldots + a\overline{X}_K) \quad (1.1)$$

The mean square or variance for the numerator of this comparison is found by formula 1.2:

$$MS_D = nD^2 / \Sigma a^2 \quad (1.2)$$

where *n* represents the number of subjects within each group (assumed here to be equal) and Σa^2 is the sum of the squared weights. The formula can be modified to accommodate unequal sample sizes (see Chapter 6).

Once the mean square for the comparison is found, it is divided by the within mean square to produce the F-statistic. The ratio is declared significant if it exceeds the value of *F* determined by the particular decision rule adopted. Again, as in the example, the assumption is made that subjects have been randomly assigned to treatment groups (i.e., that a randomized group design has been used).

2. A PRIORI COMPARISONS

In most theory-based research the experimenter knows which specific questions must be answered. These questions, which are typically limited in number, are known *before* data are collected and are thus based on *a priori* knowledge. We will concern ourselves in this chapter with the issues, methods, and illustrations used to analyze these types of experiments. A primary issue will be to determine the appropriate control to be exercised over Type I errors. Comparisons that are *orthogonal* to or independent of one another will be differentiated from those that provide redundant or correlated information.

ORTHOGONAL COMPARISONS

Comparisons may be presented either as a t-statistic or as an F-ratio with one degree of freedom in the numerator. Although the choice is largely arbitrary, this chapter will present comparisons as F-ratios. The advantages of doing so are that (1) the hypothesis being tested by the comparison is stated explicitly as a set of weights, and (2) complex comparisons involving differential weighting of treatment groups are more easily accomplished.

As noted in Chapter 1, the comparison must be expressed by a configuration of weights that represents the question under investigation and that sums to zero. These weights are multiplied by the treatment means (in some texts the treatment *sums* are used instead of the means) to yield a weighted sum symbolized by D. If the null hypothesis is true for the comparison, D will differ *randomly* from zero; if Ho is false, D will differ systematically from zero. D is then used to generate a *mean square* for that comparison:

$$MS = nD^2/\Sigma a^2 \qquad (2.1)$$

where n is the sample size for each treatment group and Σa^2 is the sum of squared weights. If the ratio between the mean square for the comparison and the mean square within groups is sufficiently greater than one, the difference being investigated by the comparison is statistically significant.

Assume that the primary question of concern is whether groups that maintain unanimous responses from the confederates differ from those groups in which one confederate deviates from the responses of the remaining confederates. The five groups are divided into the two unanimous groups (Groups I and II) and the three nonunanimous groups (Groups III, IV, and V). One set of weights that would combine and compare these two sets would have coefficients of 3, 3, –2, –2, –2 for the five groups, respectively. Note that groups that are to be combined have the same sign and that the sum of all weights is zero. An equivalent set of weights would be 1/2, 1/2, –1/3, –1/3, –1/3. While this latter set shows the averaging process more directly, the use of fractional weights makes the arithmetic more tedious.

Multiplying the treatment means by these coefficients provides the following value of D:

$$D = (3)(5.20)+(3)(5.08)+(-2)(2.44)+(-2)(3.44)+(-2)(3.76) = 11.56$$

The mean square associated with this value of D is found by using formula 2.1:

$$MS_D = \frac{(25)(11.56^2)}{30} = 111.36$$

The F-ratio associated with this MS is found by dividing the MS_D by the MS_W from the original ANOVA. This value of F is:

$$F = \frac{111.36}{5.29} = 21.05.$$

The respective degrees of freedom are 1 and 120. The decision whether or not to reject this Ho depends on the particular decision rule adopted for the experiment.

The question asked in this comparison is whether the average effect of unanimous opposition produces greater conformity than the average effect of having one dissenter within the group. The test is considerably more powerful than those used for pairwise comparisons (see Chapter 3) since the two means being compared are based on 50 and 75 subjects for the unanimous and nonunanimous groups, respectively. The potential for increases in power (because of increased sample size) is an attractive feature of planned comparisons. In most experiments having three or more treatments, the researcher has several comparisons that should be tested to explore the treatment differences more fully. The nature of the relationship between these comparisons has generally been an important determiner of the decision rule to use for the null hypothesis.

CHARACTERISTICS OF ORTHOGONAL COMPARISONS

Mutually orthogonal comparisons ask questions that are independent or uncorrelated with one another. This means that the research questions are concerned about differences that are not redundant with differences explored in other comparisons. In the conformity example the first question was concerned about the difference between the first two treatment groups and the remaining three groups. Any additional comparison that investigates a difference between one of the unanimous groups with any of the last three would be partially redundant with the first comparison and not orthogonal to it. Questions that are unrelated to the first comparison include any analysis that compares groups that were combined previously. Thus a comparison of the mean responses obtained from the 7-person unanimous treatment with the mean responses of the 4-person unanimous group would be independent of or orthogonal to the first comparison.

A simple test can indicate if two comparisons are orthogonal. The test involves multiplying the weights of the two comparisons for each treatment group and summing these products.[5] If the sum is zero, the comparisons are orthogonal. The weights for the first comparison are 3, 3,–2,–2,–2; for the comparison of the two unanimous groups (disregarding all others), the weights are 1, –1, 0, 0, 0. The orthogonality of these two comparisons can be shown in the following manner:

$$(\mathit{3})(1)+(\mathit{3})(-1)+(\mathit{-2})(0)+(\mathit{-2})(0)+(\mathit{-2})(0) = 0$$

where the first number in each product (italicized) is the weight for the first comparison, and the second number is the weight for the second comparison.

To be mutually orthogonal, additional comparisons would have to be independent of all remaining comparisons in the set. In the current example, conducting the two comparisons as described previously would restrict the only nonredundant questions to those concerning differences between Groups III, IV, and V. These differences were not analyzed in the first comparison since all three groups were summed together. In the second comparison the three groups were given zero weight.

When queried about which differences are important among the three groups with nonunanimous responses, the researcher might be interested in a number of comparisons; but once one question is asked concerning these three groups, only a single question remains that will be orthogonal to all other comparisons. For example, if theory predicts that subjects who receive the support of one other person would be able to resist conformity to a greater extent than those who were in a group having a nonsupporting person, the comparison would be between Group III (in which the subject received the support of another individual) and Groups IV and V (in which other subjects broke from the majority but did not support the subject). The appropriate weights used to analyze this question are 0, 0, 2, –1, –1. The orthogonality of this comparison with the first two can be checked by summing the products of weights for each pair of comparisons. This sum is 0 with comparisons 1 and 2.

Given these first three comparisons, there is only one question that could not overlap with one already asked. This question concerns the difference between the two groups in which a deviant but nonsupportive

TABLE 3
Analysis of Four Planned, Orthogonal Comparisons Carried Out Using the Conformity Example Data

Groups	I	II	III	IV	V			
Means	5.20	5.08	2.44	3.76	3.44			
	Comparisons					*D*	*MS*	*F*
3	3	−2	−2	−2		11.56	111.36	21.05
1	−1	0	0	0		.12	.18	<1
0	0	2	−1	−1		−2.32	22.43	4.24
0	0	0	1	−1		.32	1.28	<1

response was given. In Group IV the second confederate responded with a different incorrect response than was given by the other confederates on the 12 critical trials. In treatment V the second confederate occasionally gave incorrect answers on the noncritical trials where all other confederates gave correct responses. The difference between these two groups is tested using the weights 0, 0, 0, 1, −1; it is orthogonal to all other comparisons under consideration.

For any experiment with k treatment groups, there are k–1 comparisons that will be orthogonal to one another. With 5 treatment groups (as in the conformity experiment), it is possible to construct 4 nonredundant comparisons. Given those 4 comparisons, any additional comparison must be partially redundant with at least one of these. Although there are many sets of orthogonal comparisons, each set contains only k–1 comparisons.

A related characteristic of orthogonal comparisons is that they partition or divide the variability among the means into mutually exclusive and exhaustive parts. The sum of the variability associated with the comparisons in a complete set of k–1 orthogonal comparisons is equal to the variability found in the *between-groups sum of squares*. Because each comparison has one df, it is both a sum of squares and a mean square. The sum of the dfs for the complete set of comparisons is the number of dfs associated with the between sum of squares, k–1.

Table 3 shows that most of the variability associated with the treatments is accounted for by the difference between the groups in which all confederates provide unanimous responses compared with those groups in which there is a break in consensus. The only other comparison that accounts for sufficient variability to produce an *F* greater than 1.0 is the difference between the group in which the consensus breaker gave the same response as the subject compared with the two groups in which the confederate responded with a different but incorrect response. Whether these two comparisons are significant depends on the decision rule used in the experiment.

DECISION RULE FOR EVALUATING ORTHOGONAL COMPARISONS

The decision rule for evaluating the significance of comparisons within a set of mutually orthogonal comparisons is usually based on a 5% per comparison Type I error rate. This level of control over Type I error is more liberal than is usually recommended for multiple comparisons. When paired with the increased power obtained by combining samples from different groups, the experimenter is provided with very powerful tests to answer a few important questions. This level of control over Type I error is based on three conditions inherent with orthogonal comparisons. First, the comparisons are planned before data are collected. The experimenter is thus unable to design the comparison to capitalize on unusual but random events that might be observed within the set of means. The questions addressed by the comparisons are determined by the theory under investigation and not by the configuration of the data. Second, orthogonal comparisons involve a small number of significance tests. As noted previously, the greatest number of comparisons possible is k–1 for a set of *k* means. And third, orthogonal comparisons are, by definition, independent of one another. The numerators of the F-ratios for the comparisons are based on independent parts of the treatment variability. The probability of a Type I error on one comparison will be partially independent of that error on another comparison. Thus, if a comparison does result in a Type I error, that error is likely to be isolated and not repeated on other comparisons. The lack of complete independence is produced because all tests use a common estimate in the denominator.

Referring to Table 3, a 5% per comparison decision rule would lead to the rejection of any F-ratio greater than 3.92. Thus the researcher would reject the null hypotheses for the first and third comparisons.

STRATEGIES FOR DEVELOPING SETS OF ORTHOGONAL COMPARISONS

Although there are many possible sets of orthogonal comparisons, there are only a few general strategies for developing these sets. Presented below are three strategies that may help investigators who want to state research questions orthogonally. The value of any of these approaches depends on the extent to which the set of comparisons is appropriate to the questions asked.

The first rule is exemplified by the set of comparisons presented earlier in this chapter. Comparisons are orthogonal if one comparison *combines* treatment groups while a second comparison involves the *differences* between groups that had been combined previously. Experiments that involve this set of comparisons are called *hierarchical designs*. For example, if four instructors of a common class were paired such that one pair depended on lectures while the other depended on a more Socratic approach, the primary question might concern the difference in student achievement under these two conditions. The appropriate weights would be 1, 1, –1, –1 where the positive weights are arbitrarily assigned to the lecturing instructors and the negative weights to the Socratic pair. The comparisons that would be orthogonal to this configuration would determine if instructors within a method differ significantly from one another. Two separate comparisons are needed: one comparison between the two lecturers and one between the two Socratic instructors.

A second approach to generating orthogonal comparisons relies on different combinations of treatment groups. All groups are involved in each comparison of different groupings. Typically, the designs for which this set of comparisons are used are factorial designs with two levels of each factor. As originally described, the conformity study would *not* be analyzed appropriately with this set of comparisons. However, by redesigning the experiment we can produce a set of treatments that represent a factorial configuration that would be analyzed by this second type of comparison set. The 2×2 factorial contains the following groups:

A. 7 person groups unanimously opposed on critical trials
B. 4 person groups unanimously opposed on critical trials
C. 7 person groups with one supporter on critical trials
D. 4 person groups with one supporter on critical trials

The first question of interest is whether the groups with unanimous opposition differed from the groups having a supporter. This comparison is called "the main effect for group type." The weights for this comparison are 1, 1, –1, –1 where the positive weights refer to the unanimously opposing groups and where the negative weights are used for the groups with supporters. The second comparison involves group size. The two groups having 7 persons are given the same signed values; groups of 4 have the opposite sign (1, –1, 1, –1). This comparison is orthogonal to the first since the sum of the weighted products equals zero.

Because there are only k–1 possible orthogonal comparisons within a set of *k* means, the current example can have only three comparisons. The question that is orthogonal to the two main effects (group type and size) is the concern for the interaction between the two factors. This effect can be found by using the weights 1, –1, –1, 1.[6] Note that the pairing of the 4 groups has occurred in all possible ways (Group A with Group B for the type of group effect, with Group C for the group size effect, and with Group D for the interaction).

A third strategy used to define orthogonal sets is based on a series of tests in which one group is compared with all remaining groups and is then eliminated from any additional comparisons. This routine of isolating and then excluding is continued until only two groups remain to be compared. Usually, the experiment for which this set of comparisons is appropriate consists of treatment groups in which the complexity or number of elements with the groups increases.

We will again modify the conformity experiment to demonstrate this third strategy. The four groups are as follows:

A. 7 unanimous confederates
B. 7 confederates in which the second person provides incorrect answers on noncritical trials
C. 7 confederates where the second confederate provides an incorrect answer that differs on critical trials from the remaining confederates
D. 7 confederates where the second confederate provides the correct answer on critical trials

Placed in this order, the treatment groups should provide increasing support for the subject as reflected in decreased conforming responses. The three comparisons would be defined by the following weights:

A	B	C	D	
3	−1	−1	−1	(unanimous versus all others)
0	2	−1	−1	(break on noncritical trials versus all others)
0	0	1	−1	(break on critical trials versus support)

In many instances, such as this one, the questions posed by this third strategy are very close to the questions asked by the first strategy. In both cases the groups being compared in one set of weights were combined previously. The difference is that the third strategy always pits one group against the remaining ones; with hierarchical designs, the weights first divide the groups into two major sets and then probe within the sets for the remaining comparisons.

PROTECTION LEVELS FOR ORTHOGONAL COMPARISONS

If the 5% level per comparison is used to reject Ho for each of the k–1 comparisons in an orthogonal set, the experimentwise error rate will be considerably larger than 5%. In the set of 5 means from the original conformity study, the experimentwise error rate is one minus the probability of making all correct decisions when Ho is true. Protection against Type I errors was called a "protection level" by Duncan (1955). Although he was referring specifically to pairwise comparisons (see Chapter 3), these same considerations are relevant within a set of orthogonal comparisons. When events are independent, the probability of their joint occurrence is the product of their separate and independent probabilities.

The formula for protection level is:

$$\text{Protection level} = 1 - (1 - a)^r$$

where *a* is the alpha level used and *r* is the number of independent comparisons conducted. For a complete set of k–1 orthogonal comparisons with alpha set at .05, the protection level for the orthogonal comparisons in the conformity experiment would be:

$$\text{Protection level} = 1 - (1 - .05)^4$$
$$= .81$$

Thus the experimentwise Type I error rate would be 1 – .81 = .19.

While an independent estimate of the denominator would be needed for each comparison for the above equation to be precise, the magnitude of the values gives a reasonable indication of the probability of correctly accepting all tested null hypotheses if they were, in fact, all true.

ORTHOGONAL POLYNOMIALS

A special use of orthogonal comparisons is called *trend analysis* or *trend analyses for orthogonal polynomials*. This type of orthogonal comparison involves treatments with differing *amounts* of a variable rather than with differing *kinds* of treatments. Some examples of treatments that could be compared by trend analyses include drug studies with systematic differences in the dosage given different groups, learning studies that vary the number of trials students receive, and instructional studies with groups having different amounts of time to learn a task. These examples involve changes in the levels of the treatment effect.

An example will help to explain the rationale and computations involved in trend analyses. Although the original conformity study would not be appropriate for a trend analysis (the differences between groups are differences in *kind* and not in *amount*), a major issue in conformity is how the size of the group influences the degree of conformity. Although the original study had group sizes of 4 and 7, we can concentrate more on group size by establishing groups of size 3, 4, 5, 6, and 7 members of which all but the subject are confederates of the experimenter. The subject is always placed in the last position for groups of 3, 4, and 5, and in the next to last position for groups of 6 and 7. The confederates are coached to give a unanimous (and incorrect) response on the critical trials. Each treatment condition is run with 25 subjects. The means and their plotted locations are depicted in Figure 1.

The questions of interest to the experimenter concern the fit between a small number of idealized trends and the data. The hypothesized

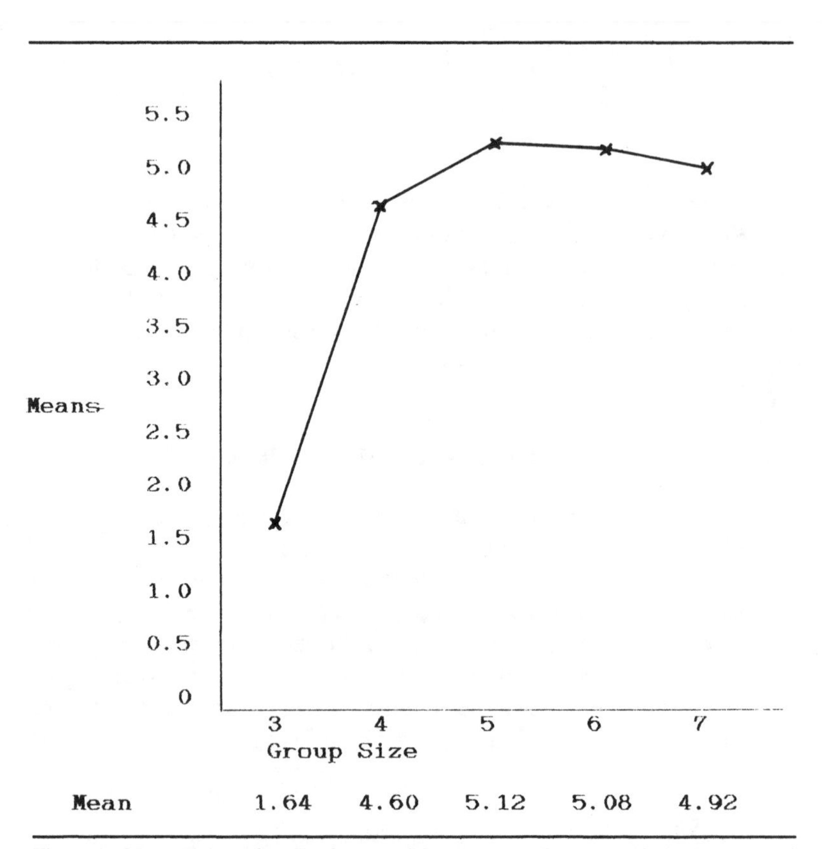

Figure 1: Mean Values for Conformity Measure as a Function of the Number of Members in a Group

trends of interest are portrayed in Figure 2, Examples A through D. Note that the number of bends in the idealized graphs distinguishes one comparison from another. The closer the model fits the observed data, the greater will be the amount of variability explained by that particular trend. If we compare Figure 1 with the idealized trend in Figure 2, we note that the trend for the 5 groups contains a strong linear component with the very low mean associated with the group with only 2 peers and the subject and the higher means for larger groups. Additionally, there is a noticeable flattening in the figure with a decrease in the larger groups. This suggests a curvature in the trend in addition to the linear trend. No more complex trends seem to be present in the data.

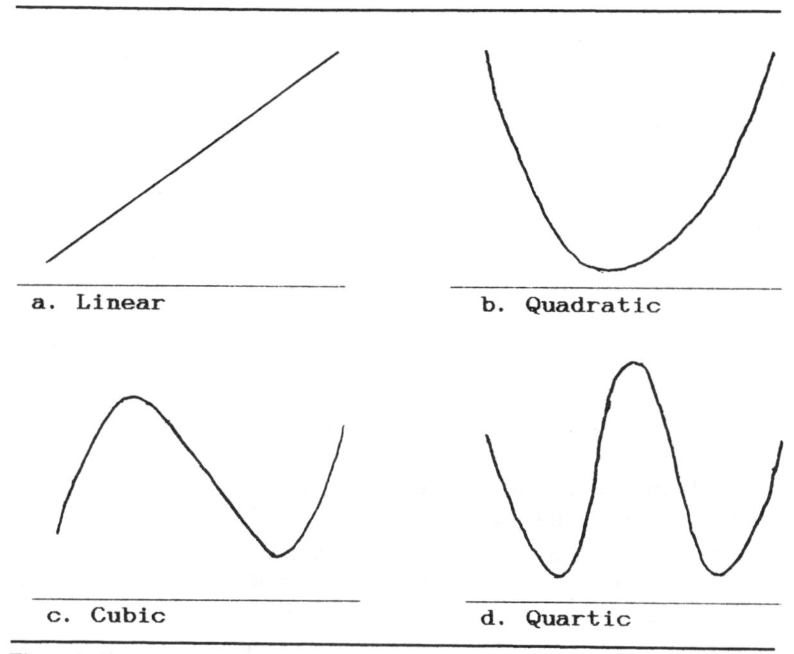

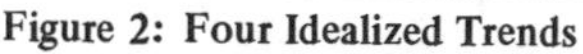

Figure 2: Four Idealized Trends

The above discussion is in anticipation of the actual tests of significance. Each of the comparisons for a trend requires a set of weights that reflect that particular trend. These weights can be found in many statistics texts, including Edwards (1985) and Keppel (1982). For 5 treatment groups the set of weights for the linear trend is –2, –1, 0, 1, 2. Note that these weights fit a model of constant change in mean levels. These weights are multiplied by the treatment means to provide a value for *D*. *D* will differ systematically from zero if the outcome means correlate with the corresponding treatment levels. The weights for a second degree or quadratic equation portray a single bend. For a set of 5 means, the quadratic coefficients or weights are 2, –1, –2, –1, 2. These coefficients are orthogonal to those for a linear trend (–2, –1, 0, 1, 2):

$$(-2)(2)+(-1)(-1)+(0)(-2)+(1)(-1)+(2)(2) = 0$$

A set of *k* treatment groups requires k–1 comparisons to account for all the variability in the treatment sum of squares. When the comparisons

TABLE 4
Summary Table for Trend Analysis Using Modified Data from Conformity Example

	I	*II*	*III*	*IV*	*V*	MS_D	*F*
Linear	–2	–1	0	1	2	123.90	20.58
Quadratic	–2	1	2	1	–2	87.57	13.72
Cubic	–1	2	0	–2	1	13.46	2.24
Quartic	1	–4	6	–4	1	0.74	< 1
Within Mean Square						6.02 (df = 120)	

are tests for trends, there are k–1 different trends needed to describe the differences between means.

As the number of groups increases, the trends can become extremely complex. Tables often provide only a portion of the possible trends for experiments with many treatments. Thus an experiment with many treatment groups might not completely partition the treatment sum of squares into the possible number of orthogonal comparisons. The available coefficients represent the simplest trends. When the treatment variability is partitioned into only the simplest trends, the remaining variability is often summed into an unanalyzed residual term with several degrees of freedom. If the F-ratio for the residual mean square indicates a significant source of variability, one or more complex trends are also significant. These complex trends may be of limited interest to the experimenter.

The expectations for the trends are borne out by the analysis. The weights used for each comparison are presented in Table 4 along with the mean squares and F-ratios for the data. Although these data are fictitious, they resemble closely the findings reported by Asch (1951) and by Gerard, Wilhelmy, and Connolley (1968). The linear portion of the treatment sum of squares is 123.90, and the quadratic is 82.57. These two effects account for 123.90 + 82.57 = 206.47 of the 220.67 treatment sum of squares. Using the within-mean square as the denominator, the linear and the quadratic effects would be significant with F-ratios at the 5% level of significance. The description of the treatment means would be that they increase with increases in group sizes, that the increase is accelerating negatively, and that there is a leveling off within the range observed.

NONORTHOGONAL COMPARISONS

In many experiments the researcher has well-defined a priori hypotheses that turn out not to be orthogonal. At the beginning of this chapter we suggested that the most important comparison of the conformity experiment might be the combination of the two unanimous groups compared with the three groups having a break in unanimity. The weights for that comparison were 3, 3, –2, –2, –2. But the researcher could also justify comparing the three groups with breaks in the unanimity of the group response with the unanimous groups of 7 persons. This comparison might be used because the researcher was concerned that group size affected the degree of conformity and thus wanted a comparison in which all groups were based on 7 people. This comparison would have the weights 3, 0, –1, –1, –1 and is not orthogonal to the first comparison as shown by the sum of the products:

$$(3)(3)+(3)(0)+(-2)(-1)+(-2)(-1)+(-2)(-1) = 15.$$

The number of nonorthogonal comparisons conducted is often small, reflecting the experimental questions of interest; but because they are partially redundant, they have led to the development of different procedures.

FIVE PERCENT PER COMPARISON ERROR RATE

One possibility for analyzing a small number of planned and correlated comparisons is to proceed as if the experimenter were analyzing an orthogonal comparison with a 5% per comparison error rate. The conditions that led to this recommendation for orthogonal comparisons generally hold true for nonorthogonal comparisons. These conditions include the following: (1) the questions under investigation are planned and therefore do not allow the researcher to capitalize on chance differences, and (2) the number of comparisons of interest to the researcher is small and therefore reduces the probability of committing Type I errors.

The experimentwise error rate for a set of planned and correlated contrasts depends on the number of comparisons to be made and the extent to which these comparisons are correlated. The maximum probability of a Type I error experimentwise is equal to the sum of the error rates on each of the comparisons. If two comparisons are of interest and if each was conducted with a 5% per comparison error rate, the experimentwise error rate must be less than 5% + 5% or 10%. This general principle concerning the experimentwise error rate is known as *Bonferroni's inequality*. If comparisons were mutually exclusive, the Type I error rate experimentwise would be the sum of the separate probabilities. In reality comparisons will not be mutually exclusive, so the actual experimentwise error rate will be less than the sum. With nonorthogonal comparisons the comparisons are partially redundant, so that a Type I error on one comparison will tend to be associated with Type I errors on other comparisons.[7] This results in the true experimentwise error rate being somewhere between the sum of the separate per comparison error rates and 5%. The lower bound of 5% is attained only in the absurd situation where all questions completely duplicate one another. In that situation the commission of a Type I error would be reflected in all comparisons.

The major difference between orthogonal and nonorthogonal comparisons involves the number of Type I errors committed within an experiment. If the tests are orthogonal, Type I errors will occur in isolation. Because the numerators are independent, when the random configuration of means results in a rejected Ho for one comparison, the remaining comparisons will combine the means so as not to capitalize on the original chance difference. With orthogonal comparisons it is possible to have more than one Type I error in a set, but admittedly that would be rare. With nonorthogonal comparisons a Type I error made on one comparison could be replicated on others within that set. Although this results in more Type I errors per experiment when an error does occur, it also results in fewer experiments that contain any errors.

DUNN'S TEST

Some researchers consider a 5% per comparison error rate as being too large. They may prefer to reduce the probability of committing an experimentwise Type I error by using a smaller value, such as a 1% per comparison error rate. If the number of comparisons is small, the result will be a tolerably small experimentwise error rate. The justification for using a 1% level is that tables for the F-distribution usually present critical values only for the 5% and 1% levels. Thus the decision is made for expediency rather than for sound statistical reasons.

A preferred way to control the probability of an experimentwise Type I error is to make use of *Bonferroni's inequality* by limiting the total Type I error rate to no more than 5%. This can be accomplished by making the sum of the per comparison error rates equal to 5%. Thus, for a planned set of *p* comparisons, the error rate per comparison would be set at .05/p. This procedure is called *Dunn's Test* (Dunn, 1961) and requires the use of a table that will divide the 5% among the various comparisons. This table can be found in numerous statistics texts, including those by Howell (1982) and Edwards (1985).

Because any comparison can be expressed as an F-ratio with one df in the numerator, Dunn's Test will be described that way, although *t* is also widely used. The use of Dunn's Test with an F-ratio requires that the observed ratio be compared with the square of the tabled t-value. This modification is permissible since $t^2 = F$.

No new formulas are needed for Dunn's Test. The MS for the comparison is calculated by using formula 2.1, and the F-ratio is formed by dividing the MS for the comparison by the MS within. The only unique feature of Dunn's Test is that the decision whether to reject Ho or not is based on critical values found in a special table first prepared by Dunn (1961). The tabled values depend on the number of degrees of freedom on which the mean square is based and on the number of comparisons that were planned.

Table 5 contains a set of comparisons for the most important research questions of interest. This set contains 6 comparisons on the 5 treatment conditions. Several of the comparisons were contained within the set that were mutually orthogonal at the beginning of this chapter. Others have been added to clarify the role of the confederate who deviates only on trials where no one else provides the incorrect response. More specifically, comparisons 5 and 6 test whether the conformity in these groups differs from those that involve the critical trials and the unanimous group, respectively. Some of the questions asked in this set are not orthogonal, as can be discerned by examining the number of questions and the redundancy in some of the comparisons.

Next to each row of weights is the mean square for the comparison and the F-ratio. When the mean square within has 120 degrees of freedom for 6 comparisons, Dunn's Test requires an *F* of 10.43 to reject Ho with no more than a 5% chance of a Type I error experimentwise. The per comparison error rate in the experiment would be .05/6 = .0083.

Two tests of significance rejected the null hypothesis. Both of these tests compared the unanimous group(s) with a combination of the other

TABLE 5
Planned, Nonorthogonal Comparisons Performed on Conformity Example Data

I	*II*	*III*	*IV*	*V*	*D*	MS_D	*F*
3	3	−2	−2	−2	11.56	111.36	22.18
1	−1	0	0	0	.12	.18	<1
0	0	2	−1	−1	−2.32	22.43	4.47
2	0	−1	−1	0	14.52	85.13	16.96
0	0	1	1	−2	−1.64	11.21	2.23
1	0	0	0	−1	1.44	25.92	5.16

groups. The only test of significance that compared the unanimous group of 7 with nonunanimous responses was comparison 6, which was not significant.

An important point to keep in mind when basing the error rate on the number of comparisons to be conducted is that this number is based on the planned, total number of tests being contemplated. Consider two examples. In the first the researcher plans on 3 comparisons, realizes that the means are virtually identical on one comparison, and as a result decides to disregard that comparison. In the second example the researcher plans for 3 comparisons but after collecting data realizes that the pattern of means suggests a fourth comparison. Both researchers are creating serious problems concerning the probability of Type I errors. In the first example the experimenter must still base the error rate on the original set of *three* planned comparisons. In the second example the decision to run additional tests resulted from an examination of the data. The appropriate control over Type I errors in this situation requires the use of the *Scheffé Test*, which will be described more fully in Chapter 4.

SUMMARY AND RECOMMENDATIONS

Our recommendation is to use a 5% per comparison error rate when the number of comparisons is small. This recommendation holds for both orthogonal and nonorthogonal comparisons. However, when the number of planned comparisons exceeds the number of degrees of freedom in the mean square between groups, the recommendation is to use either Dunn's procedure or the Scheffé Test (see Chapter 4), whichever is the more powerful for the situation at hand. This need for increased conservatism is prompted by the apparent inability or unwillingness of the investigator to generate a limited number of hypotheses and comparisons. As these numbers increase, the implication also increases that the experimenter had decided to "milk the data" in the search for *any* significant differences instead of trying to think the problem through *before* data collection was begun. If researchers want to depend on the vague hope that serendipitous findings can be relied on, the "penalty" will be that more conservative tests may have to be used.

Sometimes an experimenter may have a small number of comparisons planned for an experiment but may also want to examine the differences between groups for which specific hypotheses were not made. In these cases a combination of the procedures described in this chapter and those to be described in Chapters 3 and 4 may be appropriate. The critical concern is that the post hoc comparisons be on previously unanalyzed differences between groups.

3. POST HOC COMPARISONS: PAIRWISE METHODS

This chapter describes procedures for testing differences between all pairs of means within an experiment. Pairwise comparisons are designed to address all possible combinations of the treatment groups. No comparison is set aside as being more interesting or important than any others. The experimenter who performs pairwise comparisons is assuming that all differences between means are important and of theoretical interest; there is no provision for tests of combinations of groups.

Chapter 2 discussed *planned comparisons* in which theory predicts that some treatment groups will produce similar effects that are, in turn, different from other treatments. Although it might be possible to detect patterns in the results by observing which differences are significant and which are not, the evaluation of a priori hypotheses concerning combinations of treatment groups is an inappropriate use of pairwise comparisons.

Referring to the conformity example, the experimenter reasonably could analyze the results by using pairwise comparisons. If this option were selected, the experimenter examines the differences between each of the groups to determine which of the varying demands for conformity produced different effects. Once the choice has been made to examine differences between each pair of means, a second decision is necessary concerning the appropriate control over Type I error.

This chapter describes five tests that define different decision rules for pairwise comparisons. Four of these tests use the range statistic q; the other test is a variation of a t-test.

RATIONALE FOR RANGE TESTS

The null hypothesis for a range test is that all means within a set are drawn from a common population. If this hypothesis is true, the difference between the largest and smallest sample means is judged to be due to chance effects. Because the difference between the two extreme means depends on the particular subjects who were assigned randomly to the groups, that difference is subject to random fluctuation from one set of means to another. If many sets of means were drawn—each with the same sample size and number of means—the difference between the largest and smallest elements would vary from one set to another. The sampling distribution of the distance between means is known and is standardized by dividing the difference by the standard error of the mean. This statistic (symbolized by q) forms the basis for range tests.

SAMPLING DISTRIBUTION OF RANGES

The sampling distribution of the standardized range is a function of the number of means within the set and the number of degrees of freedom on which the standard error is based. In any sample of elements, including a sample of means, the more elements that are sampled, the more likely it is that an unusual event will occur. If many sample means are drawn, the effects of random sampling will result in one or more means having relatively small values, while other samples will have large values. This will produce a large range between the outermost means simply because of the number of means within the set. With fewer means there are fewer opportunities to observe unusually large or small sample means; thus, on the average, a small number of means will produce a shorter range between the extreme means.

The second factor to influence the standardized range is the number of degrees of freedom on which the standard error of the mean is based. If the standard error is derived from a variance estimate that is based on just a few degrees of freedom, the magnitude of the standard error would vary greatly from one sample of observations to another. When the standard error is overestimated, the range will tend to decrease; if underestimated, the standard error will result in larger values for the standardized range. The critical information about the sampling distribution for the range test is the point at which the largest alpha proportion of the sampling distribution begins. When the standard error of the mean is unstable because of the few number of degrees of freedom employed, some ranges will be divided by estimates of the standard error that are considerably smaller than the corresponding population value and result in large values of q. Thus, when the standard error is based on a small number of degrees of freedom, the largest alpha proportion of the values of q will have numerical values that are greater than would have been found had the standard error been based on more degrees of freedom.

The first step in any range test is to order the means from smallest to largest. Tables are available that describe the value of q that is required to be one of the largest alpha percent of those that occur by chance. If the value of q calculated from the conformity experiment is greater than the tabled value, we reject Ho that all groups are drawn from the same population and conclude instead that the largest and smallest means come from different populations. The tests then proceed to ask whether subsets of the treatment means were drawn from a common population. The Ho about the partial set of means between the span of the two most extreme means is called a *partial null hypothesis*. The difference between the largest and smallest means from a subset of the groups is evaluated to determine if it reflects more variability than would be expected by chance. If so, the test proceeds to evaluate smaller subsets. Most of the methods halt the process when a subset of means is found that does not reject Ho. If the largest and smallest means cannot reject Ho, none of the means between these two extremes would lead logically to a rejected Ho.

When applied to the conformity experiment data from Table 1, the range tests all rely on the value of q, which is calculated from formula 3.1:

$$q = \frac{\overline{X}_{largest} - \overline{X}_{smallest}}{s_{\overline{X}}} \quad (3.1)$$

where $\overline{X}_{largest}$ and $\overline{X}_{smallest}$ are the two extreme means within the set. For the full Ho these are the largest and smallest means within the experiment. For partial null hypotheses q is based on the largest and smallest means within a subset. The standard error of the mean (s_x) is defined as:

$$s_{\overline{X}} = \sqrt{\frac{MS_{within}}{n}}$$

where MS_{within} is the within mean square from the analysis of variance, and n is the number of subjects within each sample. The within mean square from Table 1 is 5.29, which produces a standard error of:

$$s_{\overline{X}} = \sqrt{\frac{5.29}{25}} = 0.46$$

Because the MS_w was based on df = 120, the appropriate q distribution also has 120 dfs.

TABLE 6
Pairwise Differences for the Data in the Conformity Experiment

Means

III 2.44 V 3.44 IV 3.76 II 5.08 I 5.20

Group Comparisons	*Mean Difference*	*q*	*Range*	*t*
I-III	2.76	6.00	5	4.24
I-V	1.76	3.83	4	2.71
II-III	2.64	5.74	4	4.06
I-IV	1.44	3.13	3	2.21
II-V	1.64	3.57	3	2.52
IV-III	1.32	2.87	3	2.03
I-II	0.12	0.26	2	0.18
II-IV	1.32	2.87	2	2.03
IV-V	0.32	0.70	2	0.49
V-III	1.00	2.17	2	1.54

The necessary information for all of the range tests is presented in Table 6. Column 1 presents the pair of means being compared; column 2, the difference between the means; and column 3 presents the corresponding value of q. The fourth column indicates the number of means or range for each comparison. The last column contains the value of t for the pair that will be discussed later in the chapter. At the bottom of the table are the means from Table 1 arranged in ascending order.

Having all of the values of q, the only remaining issue is to determine whether a particular value is sufficiently large to reject Ho for that set of means. Each of the procedures discussed will develop a different decision rule that dictates when the null hypothesis should be rejected. The first procedure to be discussed is Tukey's Honestly Significant Difference (HSD) Test.

TUKEY'S HONESTLY SIGNIFICANT DIFFERENCE TEST (HSD)

Tukey's *Honestly Significant Difference Test* (HSD) is the most conservative pairwise comparison test in that it exercises the greatest control over the erroneous rejection of Ho. Because of this conservative stance, it is also the least powerful of the pairwise comparisons. This lack of power means that the HSD is the least likely test to detect real differences between pairs of means.

The HSD decision rule for accepting or rejecting Ho is to reject Ho if the observed value lies within the largest 5% of the sampling distribution of studentized ranges for k means. For any of the $k(k-1)/2$ or 10 possible pairs of means to be declared significant, the difference must exceed the 5% level for a set of k (or, in this example, 5) means. The same standard or critical value is retained for every comparison.

The critical value used in the HSD test of significance ensures that the probability of incorrectly rejecting Ho does not exceed 5%. Thus, if Ho is true and all groups were, in fact, sampled from the same population, the probability would be no more than .05 that any of the pairs of means incorrectly rejected Ho. The error rate *experimentwise* is 5%.

To complete the analysis, a table of q distributions must be used. This table may be found in numerous statistics books, including Ferguson (1981) and Keppel (1982). From this table we obtain the value of q needed to mark off the largest 5% of the q values when there are 5

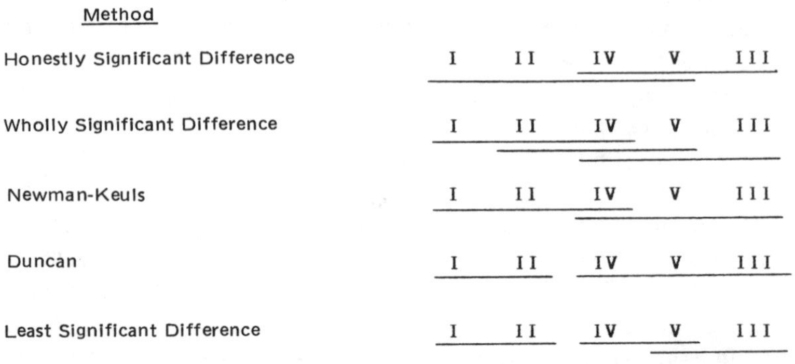

Method					
Honestly Significant Difference	I	II	IV	V	III
Wholly Significant Difference	I	II	IV	V	III
Newman-Keuls	I	II	IV	V	III
Duncan	I	II	IV	V	III
Least Significant Difference	I	II	IV	V	III

Figure 3: Summary of Findings for Different Pairwise Comparison Methods Using Conformity Experiment Data

treatment groups (as in our example), and the variance is based on 120 dfs. This point in the *q* distribution has a value of 3.92. That is, if 5 samples were drawn repeatedly from the same population, the value of *q* would exceed 3.92 only 5% of the time. The HSD Test requires any comparison to be declared significant to be one of the largest 5% that would occur by chance. Thus an observed value of *q* must exceed 3.92 to be declared significant in the present example.

Of the 10 possible comparisons among the 5 treatment means, only 2 exceed 3.92. These 2 are the differences between Groups I and III and between Groups II and III. All of the remaining differences are too small to reject Ho. These results are summarized in the first row of Figure 3. The other rows contain findings from other methods discussed in this chapter and will be referred to in their appropriate sections. The top of Figure 3 contains the 5 means listed in descending order. Underlines are placed below groups that do *not* differ significantly from one another. Note that Groups III, IV, and V are connected by a single underline and that Groups I, II, IV, and V are connected by a second underline. The only pairs of means not connected by a common underline are Groups I and III and Groups II and III. The unconnected groups differ significantly between or among themselves.

NEWMAN-KEULS TEST

The Newman-Keuls method (Newman,1939; Keuls, 1952), like other pairwise comparisons, evaluates differences within a set of means. A rejected Ho for the most extreme range indicates that the largest and smallest means are unlikely to have been drawn from the same population. The researcher also needs to determine if all but one of the means may have come from a common population. The Newman-Keuls procedure evaluates *partial null hypotheses* in a manner parallel to the original Ho.

The critical value required to reject a partial Ho is based on the expected random variability of q for the number of groups currently within the partial Ho. Hence, for the tests to determine if the remaining sets of k–1 means could be considered as having come from a common population, the critical value would be based on the expected random variability of a set of k–1 means. Since the expected random variability of q is less for smaller numbers of elements, the critical values from the q tables will be smaller for a set of k–1 means than for a set of k means. If the partial Ho is rejected for k–1 groups, the process is continued with smaller subsets until sets of only 2 means are considered.

The primary difference between the Newman-Keuls and Tukey's HSD is that the critical values for Tukey remain constant for any two means regardless of the total number of means in the set. For the Newman-Keuls, the critical values reflect the partial Ho under consideration. The changing of the critical values required for partial null hypotheses necessitates the decision rule that no tests of significance may be conducted within the boundaries of nonsignificant ranges. Since a lower value of q is required for a range of k–1 means than for k means, it is conceivable that the wider range might fail to reject Ho and that a shorter range could exceed the reduced critical value. This situation is avoided by the decision rule to stop testing for additional comparisons once an insignificant range is detected.

In the conformity example described previously and presented in Table 1, the first significance test would divide the difference between the largest and smallest means by the standard error of the mean to obtain q. This is the difference between Groups I and III. From Table 3 we find the q value for this difference to be 6.00. This value of q is compared with the tabled value of 3.92 that is based on 5 means and 120 degrees of freedom. Because the observed value of q exceeds the tabled value, Ho is rejected. Had the difference produced a q that was smaller than 3.92, Ho would not have been rejected, and the analysis would have been concluded.

Because the overall Ho was rejected, the Newman-Keuls test compares the partial Ho concerning the ranges of k–1 or 4 means. For the test of the range between Groups I and V, the observed difference is

TABLE 7
Critical Values of q Required for Each Pairwise Comparison Method Using the Conformity Experiment Data (alpha = .05)

	Range			
Method	*5*	*4*	*3*	*2*
Honestly Significant Difference	3.92	3.92	3.92	3.92
Wholly Significant Difference	3.92	3.80	3.64	3.36
Newman-Keuls	3.92	3.68	3.36	2.80
Duncan	3.12	3.05	2.95	2.80
Least Significant Difference*	2.80	2.80	2.80	2.80

*Transformed from a t-statistic.

1.76 points (5.20–3.44), and the value of q for this comparison is 3.83. When 4 means are sampled with 120 degrees of freedom, the largest 5% of the q values for a true Ho are greater than 3.68, and the partial Ho is rejected. The means for Groups I and V are sufficiently far apart that it would be unlikely that they were drawn from a common population.

A similar test is conducted on the other range of 4 means, Groups II-III. Table 7 shows that the value of $q_{II\text{-}III} = 5.74$. This range also involves 4 means, and the tabled value again is 3.68. The partial Ho for the II to III range is rejected.

So far all of the ranges have produced significant differences. Each range of 4 means yields two possible ranges of 3 means. Within the I to V range (I, II, IV, V), for example, are the 3 mean ranges of I, II, IV and II, IV, V. The II to III range (II, IV, V, III) contains the ranges II, IV, V and IV, V, III. The II, IV, V range is included in both sets. The three unique ranges of 3 means will require values of q that exceed the tabled range for three means. That q value is 3.36. The values of q calculated for this example are $q_{I\text{-}IV} = 3.13$; $q_{II\text{-}V} = 3.56$; and $q_{IV\text{-}III} = 2.87$. Because the ranges from I to IV and from IV to III are not significant, the partial null hypotheses within these ranges are not tested for significance. Because all ranges of 2 means fall within one of these nonsignificant ranges, there are no further tests permitted. Had a range of 2 been conducted, it would have required a q value of 2.80 to reject the partial Ho.

The results of these tests of significance are summarized in Figure 3. The underlined means are those that do not differ significantly from one another. The first line is based on the nonsignificant difference between Groups I and IV; the second line is under Groups IV, V, and III. The same rule regarding underlining is followed with the Newman-Keuls

Test as was described previously for Tukey's HSD Test: groups *not* connected by a common underline differ significantly from one another.

TUKEY'S WHOLLY SIGNIFICANT DIFFERENCE TEST (WSD)

Tukey's HSD Test maintains the same critical value to reject Ho. In contrast, the Newman-Keuls Test varies the critical value depending on the number of groups contained within the set being compared in a partial Ho. The Type I error rate for the Newman-Keuls is retained at 5% for each of the partial null hypotheses; the error rate for partial null hypotheses is less than 5% for Tukey's HSD.

Tukey has recommended a compromise between the .05 level for the partial Ho and the more conservative HSD test that he had proposed earlier. Tukey's less conservative method is known as the *Wholly Significant Difference* (WSD) Test, which creates intermediate critical values that are the average of those used by the HSD and the Newman-Keuls. These intermediate critical values are used to evaluate the observed values of q.

The values of q are presented in Table 6 for the conformity experiment described previously. A critical value of 3.92 was required for Tukey's HSD for all differences. When this value is averaged with those provided by the Newman-Keuls test, the critical ranges are 3.92 for a range of 5 means; 3.80 for a range of 4 means; 3.64 for 3 means; and 3.36 for a range of 2 means. Differences that exceed their critical values in this example are those between the means of Groups I and III, Groups I and V, and Groups II and III. These findings are summarized in the second row of Figure 3.

THE DUNCAN TEST

Duncan (1955) has developed an alternative to the pairwise range tests that have been described so far. Although the method has greater power to detect differences, the cost of this power is decreased control over the experimentwise Type I error rate. Central to the understanding of Duncan's test is the notion of a *protection level.* The protection level of a test is the probability that a completely true Ho will lead to no erroneously rejected Ho. The protection level is the complement of the experimentwise Type I error rate. Both of Tukey's methods and the Newman-Keuls have experimentwise error rates of 5%. Duncan has argued that this level is too stringent (i.e., more conservative) than other multiple comparison tests.

More specifically, Duncan has recommended that the protection level for a series of pairwise comparisons be set at the same value as the protection level typically used when a complete set of independent comparisons is conducted. In Chapter 2 we found that there are k–1 orthogonal (independent) comparisons possible in an experiment consisting of *k* means. The usual procedure is to tolerate an alpha level (usually 5%) as the Type I error rate for each of the independent comparisons. The protection level for k–1 independent comparisons, each with an alpha chance of committing a Type I error, is found as shown in formula 3.2 below:

$$\text{Protection Level} = (1-a)^{k-1} \tag{3.2}$$

This protection against Type I errors within the experiment is the level that Duncan recommends for the experimentwise error rate for pairwise comparisons. Duncan's Test involves the same sequence rule as followed by the Newman-Keuls Test and Tukey's HSD. Thus, if the widest range does not reject Ho, no further tests are conducted. The experimentwise error rate (when the complete Ho is true) is the probability that the widest range will be rejected incorrectly. The probability of a Type I error on the widest range is, therefore, one minus the desired protection level.

If the Ho is rejected for the widest range, the significance tests are conducted on the ranges involving one fewer mean. For these and for subsequent tests, the appropriate protection for Duncan's test is shown below:

$$\text{Protection Level} = (1-a)^{r-1} \tag{3.3}$$

where *r* is the number of means contained within a given partial Ho. The critical value of *q* for any range of *r* means yields an alpha level that is one minus the protection level for that number of means. Tables that present the values of *q* needed for different values of *r* may be found in Edwards (1985). Duncan presents an additional argument for reducing the level of protection against Type I errors when many groups are being compared. Type I errors can occur only when samples are drawn from populations having a common mean. As the number of treatment groups increases, the opportunities also increase for Ho to be false.

The procedures followed in computing Duncan's Test are the same as those followed by the Newman-Keuls procedure. The only difference lies in the value used to decide whether a difference is significant or not. The widest range is evaluated against an Ho that all groups were sampled from the same population.

Using the group conformity experiment as an example and assuming an alpha level of .05, the difference between the two extreme groups represents a range of 5 means. The protection level, therefore, is $(1-.05)^{5-1} = .8145$. The initial experimentwise error rate is $1-.8145 = .1855$. From a table of q values provided by Edwards (1985), the critical value needed to reject Ho for a range of 5 means with 120 dfs is 3.12. The sampling distribution of the q statistic between the largest and smallest of 5 groups having a variance with 120 dfs indicates that 18.55% of the possible statistics have values of q greater than 3.12. The q statistic calculated for the difference between Groups I and III is 6.00, which exceeds the critical value of 3.12 and is, therefore, statistically significant. Note that q is declared to be significant at the 5% level even though the actual probability of a Type I error is .1855.

Because the largest range of 5 means was significant, the range of 4 means may then be tested. Had the largest range not been significant, no further tests would have been conducted. After Ho is rejected for all k groups, a revised Ho is defined concerning the $k-1$ means. For those null hypotheses the protection level is $(1-.05)^{4-1} = .8574$. This value is equal to a Type I error rate of .1426. The tabled value for this comparison is 3.05. The values of q for the ranges of 4 means are 3.83 for the difference between Groups I and IV and 5.74 for the difference between Groups II and III. Both of these qs exceed the critical value of 3.05 and result in rejected null hypotheses.

A range of 3 means has a protection level of $(1-.05)^{3-1} = .9025$, and the corresponding Type I error rate is .0975. The tabled value of q for a range of 3 means and 120 dfs is 2.95. The q values of 3.13 for Groups I-IV and 3.56 for Groups II-V both exceed the tabled value and are declared significant. The difference between Groups IV and III ($q = 2.87$) is smaller than the tabled value. Thus the Ho cannot be rejected for groups IV through III. Neither of the two mean ranges nested within the IV-III range (i.e., IV-V and V-III) would be tested for significance.

Still in question are the differences between the two mean ranges I-II and II-IV. The protection level for the two group comparisons is $(1-.05)^{2-1} = .95$, with an associated Type I error rate of .05. With df = 120, the tabled critical value needed to reject Ho is 2.80. The *q* values are q_{I-II} = .26 and q_{II-IV} = 2.87. The I-II difference is too small to allow the rejection of Ho, whereas the difference between Groups II and IV is sufficiently large to reject Ho. These results are depicted in Figure 3, fourth row. One underline is drawn between the two unanimous groups (I and II), and the second is drawn between the three groups in which some disagreement occurred among the peers (Groups IV, V, and III). As noted previously, all groups not connected by a common underline differ significantly from one another.

LEAST SIGNIFICANT DIFFERENCE TEST (LSD)

The *Least Significant Difference Test* (LSD) is not a range test but a procedure for comparing all possible pairs of means following the rejection of the overall Ho. Each difference between pairs of means in an experiment consisting of $k>2$ means is divided by the *standard error of the difference between means* to produce a t-statistic. This statistic is compared with the values in a t-table using a 5% per comparison error rate. A slight modification of the ordinary t-test occurs in that the within-mean square is used as the estimate of the raw score variance rather than a pooled estimate based only on the groups being compared in a specific test. Since the within-mean square is a pooled estimate based on all treatment groups, it will be more stable than estimates that are based on only 2 groups, assuming that all group variances are estimates of a common population variance. The formula for the standard error of the difference between means is:

$$S_{\bar{X}_1 - \bar{X}_2} = \sqrt{2MS_W/n} \qquad (3.4)$$

where *n* is the number of subjects in each of the treatment groups.

The importance of the original test of significance cannot be overemphasized with the LSD Test. Without the requirement that the overall Ho be rejected before the LSD is computed, the probability of a Type I error within a set of *k* means would be unacceptably large. By requiring that differences between groups be significant, the experiment-wise error rate is reduced to 5%. The major weakness of this method concerns partially true null hypotheses. In a set of 5 means, for example, if only one of the means is sampled from a different population, the LSD test would have a probability of approximately .20 of committing Type I errors in testing differences among the remaining 4 treatment groups.[8]

In the group conformity example the differences between the means are divided by the standard error of the difference between means as given in formula 3.4. This value is

$$S_{\bar{x}_1 - \bar{x}_2} = \sqrt{2(5.29)/25} = .65$$

Because the overall F-test is significant, the pairwise comparisions would be tested. The critical value of *t* (obtained from any statistics text) with df = 120 is 1.98. The differences between the means and the t-values for each pair of means are presented in Table 7. The differences range from t = 4.24 (for the difference between the unanimous group of 7 and the group in which one person supported the correct answer) to 0.49 for the difference between Groups IV and V (Group IV has one subject who is deviant on critical trials; Group V, in contrast, involves one subject who is deviant on noncritical trials). Of the 10 possible tests of significance, 7 would result in differences that are sufficiently large to reject the null hypothesis if alpha were set at .05. Summarizing the findings in the fifth row of Figure 3, the difference between Groups I and II is underlined to indicate a nonsignificant difference; differences between Groups IV and V, and V and III are also nonsignificant, as indicated in the underlining in Figure 3.

PAIRWISE COMPARISONS AND TYPE I ERROR

The five procedures for testing the differences between pairs of means have different criteria for judging how Type I error will be defined. Considering these differences, it should not be surprising that the conclusions derived from these methods may differ. Although we have considered each row in Figure 3 separately, we now turn our attention to the figure as a whole.

If HSD were used to analyze these data, the only differences declared significant would be those between Groups I or II and Group III.

Groups in which there is unanimous opposition produce significantly more conformity than groups in which one other peer member supports the subject's responses. All other differences are too small to reject their respective null hypotheses.

If less conservative methods are used, however, the number of significant findings increases. With the WSD Test the difference between Groups I and V is included among the significant differences found when the HSD Test was used by itself. The interpretation of these differences is that large groups (i.e., 7) that display unanimous opposition to the subject (Group I) respond differently from those groups that contain a single supporter (Group III) and those that provide incorrect responses on some noncritical trials (Group V). The mean responses for Groups II and V do not result in the decision to reject Ho using Tukey's WSD Test. However, if the experimenter used the criteria proposed by Newman and Keuls, the differences between Groups II and V would have been significant.

Duncan's Test is less conservative than other range tests. The effect of this conservatism is that significant differences would have been found among Groups I and IV, II and IV, and II and V. A summary of findings using the Duncan Test is that the two unanimous groups form one cluster, whereas a second group would be formed by those in which the peers were not united. No differences are significant within this second group.

The Least Significant Difference Test is the least conservative of the range tests. In addition to the differences found by the other methods, the LSD would also have declared Groups IV and III to differ significantly. This is the only finding by any method that does not involve a unanimous group with one in which some dissension exists. In Group IV the peer disagreed with the remaining confederates but did not support the correct response given by the subject; in Group III the peer agreed with the naive experimental subject.

In any test of significance it is important to remember that the researcher may either reject or fail to reject Ho. One does not demonstrate the equality of groups when a statistical test fails to reject the null hypothesis. In multiple comparisons this rule is particularly important since the failure to observe it can leave the experimenter with a set of logically inconsistent findings. For instance, the LSD Test found Group IV to differ significantly from Group III, but neither of these groups differed significantly from Group V. But if Groups IV and III estimate different population means, Group V must either differ from IV or Group III or both. The inability of the test of significance to clarify the appropriate location of Group V is a function of the power of the test. If the experimenter increased the power through larger sample size or a design that reduced the random variability, the proper grouping of means should be found.

The differences in the findings for the various methods emphasize the importance of understanding the relationship between the decision rules adopted and the decisions made. If a conservative test is adopted, there will be fewer significant findings and a greater chance to commit a Type II error between the smaller differences. More liberal tests will yield more significant differences with fewer Type II errors, but the cost will be greater susceptibility to Type I errors. The researcher has no way of knowing if, for example, the rejected Ho found by Duncan's Test and the LSD Test represent Type I errors or not; similarly, it will not be possible to determine if the failure to reject Ho with Tukey's Test or the Newman-Keuls represents a Type II error.

COMPARISONS OF PAIRWISE METHODS

At this point it will be instructive to examine the comparisons of means at three differing levels of proximity within a given set of comparisons. These three levels include the *omnibus* test for the widest range, tests of *intermediate* ranges, and tests for *ordered adjacent* means.

The methods described in this chapter rely on or can be converted to a studentized range.[9] Table 7 presents the studentized ranges that would have to be attained to reject the null hypothesis for each of the methods presented. This table was derived from the number of groups being compared and the number of degrees of freedom available in the example. Methods that require larger values of q can be described as being *conservative*, while those requiring relatively shorter ranges are described as being *liberal.*

OMNIBUS TESTS

Table 7 provides the critical values for a range of 5 with df = 120 as in the conformity example. Three methods—the Honestly Significant Difference Test (HSD), the Wholly Significant Difference Test (WSD), and the Newman-Keuls (N-K)—require the same value of q (i.e., 3.92) using a 5% experimentwise error rate. Duncan's Test and the Least Significant

Difference Test (LSD) require considerably smaller values of q to reject the null hypothesis that the treatment groups were drawn randomly from the same population.

The importance of the original Ho can be shown most clearly by reference to the LSD Test. The liberal aspect of the LSD test is offset by its requirement that the overall Ho be rejected prior to conducting the comparisons. Differences between the two most extreme means would not be conducted if there were insufficient variance between the treatment means to reject Ho (i.e., that they were all drawn from the same population). This condition reduces the experimentwise error rate for the complete Ho to 5%.

In range tests the test for the widest range is sufficient as an omnibus test of the equality of all population means without referring to the F-ratio for treatment differences. For the three conservative methods, requiring that the F-ratio (for treatment differences) and the q-statistic (for the widest range) *both* be among the most extreme 5% before rejecting Ho places a double burden on the experiment. By using both standards, the probability of committing a Type I error would be less than 5%. This decrease in probability occurs because the random configurations that result in Type I errors using F are not necessarily the same configurations that would result in Type I errors using q. Although unusually large differences in the means will tend to produce Type I errors for either test statistic, the F-ratio will be particularly large when several of the groups deviate from the overall average, while the q-statistic depends on the variability of only the two extreme means.

For the Duncan Test the effects of requiring a significant treatment effect before its use would drastically alter its liberal nature. Instead of having an experimentwise error rate based on the protection level, the error rate would be 5%.

INTERMEDIATE RANGES

The test of significance for intermediate ranges provides the greatest variety in control over Type I error. Table 7 shows that each method requires a different critical value before Ho can be rejected. The most conservative and liberal methods are the HSD and LSD Tests, respectively. The comparison of the error rates is confounded by the prior decisions that dictate whether the tests on the intermediate ranges will be conducted. The Newman-Keuls, Duncan, and Tukey's WSD require that the widest ranges be significant before the intermediate ranges are tested; the LSD Test requires a preliminary rejection of the overall Ho. Only Tukey's HSD Test has no prior requirement to test intermediate ranges, although it is futile to continue testing with equal values of *n* once a nonsignificant range is found.

The methods vary considerably with regard to their associated error rates if we disregard the potential effects of different decision rules and limit ourselves to the evaluation of the likelihood that an observed value of *q* exceeds the tabled value when the partial Ho is true. Using the values for the range of 4 means, the error rate for the decision is 5% using the N-K; the more conservative Tukey Tests (WSD and HSD) would yield Type I error rates of 4% and 3%, respectively; the more liberal Duncan Test would yield a probability of .14 of obtaining a Type I error for the partial Ho; and the LSD would yield a probability of .20 of obtaining a Type I error.[10]

A particularly interesting result can occur if the researcher deliberately imposes within the experiment an additional treatment group that is known to produce dramatically different results. Although the inclusion of this "obviously different" group would not provide much "practical" information, it could affect the outcomes of the other comparisons. If, for example, the experimenter were using either of Tukey's procedures, the inclusion of this additional group would require a large increase in the value of *q* not only for those comparisons involving the extreme group (which, of course, would be expected) but for *all* other comparisons as well. Thus the partial Ho concerning the differences between the treatment groups of interest would have a lower probability of being rejected by the inclusion of that one extreme group. On the other hand, the use of the LSD Test under the same conditions would ensure the rejection of the original Ho. In turn, this rejection would allow the intermediate comparisons to be conducted with extremely liberal control over Type I error. However, neither the Duncan Test nor the Newman-Keuls Test would be affected by the inclusion of that extreme comparison group. The tests of the partial Ho would be the same whether or not wider ranges had been included. The difference between these two methods would be in the control over Type I error, with N-K maintaining the level at 5% for *any* partial null hypothesis.

ADJACENT MEANS

For testing adjacent means within the serial listing, the N-K, LSD, and Duncan's tests require the same critical value of 5% per comparison.

The critical value for HSD is unaffected by the ordering of the comparison means, and it remains constant for all comparisons within a given experiment. As noted previously, Tukey's WSD is a compromise between the HSD and the other pairwise comparisons.

The tests for adjacent means—like those used for intermediate ranges—are affected by the number of groups in the original experiment and the decision rules that state when differences may be tested. Although the N-K, LSD, and Duncan Tests require the same difference to declare a comparison significant, they differ considerably on whether the comparison would be conducted at all. In the example the difference between Groups II and IV exceeds the critical value listed in Table 7 for the N-K, Duncan, and LSD tests. However, the difference would not be declared significant using the N-K method because the difference is included within a nonsignificant range.

Tests of partial null hypotheses for adjacent means lead to the "worst case" for Type I error. Three methods (LSD, N-K, and Duncan's Test) evaluate adjacent means using a 5% per comparison error rate. If an experiment consists of several pairs of means from the same population, each true partial Ho would be tested with a 5% chance of committing a Type I error. As an example, consider an experiment in which there are 6 treatment groups drawn from three populations. The "worst case" would occur if two samples were drawn from each population. If no Type II errors were committed on tests involving the wider ranges, the analysis would include three separate tests of significance on the true partial null hypotheses. *Each* of these tests would have a 5% chance of rejecting Ho, and the approximate probability of committing a Type I error *somewhere* within the analysis would be 5% + 5% + 5% = 15%.

Reviewing Figure 3, it is clear that the "Results" of an experiment using pairwise comparisons can change dramatically depending on the advantages and disadvantages of the particular method chosen. Although there is a lack of agreement among statisticians regarding which specific pairwise comparison to recommend in a given circumstance, we generally favor the use of the Newman-Keuls Test. This preference arises from our consideration of the relative importance of power, the clarity and simplicity of Type I error definition, and its insensitivity to the manipulation of treatment effects by the inclusion or exclusion of extreme groups. N-K is the only test that maintains the probability of a Type I error at a constant rate regardless of the range between means.

No test is appropriate under all conditions. Some of the "significant" findings for the more liberal methods may well be the result of Type I errors; similarly, some of the "nonsignificant" differences brought about by the more conservative tests may be due to Type II errors. Unfortunately, one can never be certain that either error has been committed. Instead, the method selected by the experimenter should reflect the relative concerns for these kinds of error. Our recommendation favoring the Newman-Keuls Test is made in spite of the increased Type I error rate under "worst case" conditions, primarily because other multiple-comparison tests also allow a per comparison error rate for independent tests. The exception to our recommendation occurs whenever sample sizes differ greatly from group to group or the assumptions of the test are clearly violated. In these instances Tukey's HSD can be recommended. Violations of assumptions and their effects will be discussed in greater detail in Chapter 6.

DUNNETT'S TEST

The methods presented in this chapter have tested all possible pairs of means for significance. Although some procedures are terminated before all pairs are tested, the interest is on the entire set of possible pairs. However, Dunnett (1955) has developed a test that is also concerned with pairs of means, but it differs from other procedures discussed in this chapter in that it is concerned with a *subset* of the possible pairs of means. That subset consists of the comparisons of each treatment mean with the mean of a control group.

Like the LSD Test, the Dunnett Test is expressed as a t-statistic. The standard error of the difference between means is found using the pooled within-mean square and the sample sizes from the treatment and control groups. The observed difference between the means is divided by the standard error to find the value of t. This t-value is then compared with a special table to determine whether the null hypothesis (i.e., that the treatment and control groups are drawn from the same population) should be rejected. The table constructed by Dunnett controls the experimentwise error rate at 5%. Thus, for the entire set of comparisons involving treatment and control groups, the probability of finding any incorrectly rejected null hypothesis is 5%.

To maintain the experimentwise error rate at 5%, the critical value for Dunnett's Test increases with an increase in the number of groups. In the situation where one treatment group is compared with a single control group, the critical value would correspond exactly to the value of the standard t-test. As more treatment groups are included in the study, the critical value required of any one has to increase to retain the overall Type I error rate at 5%.

An experimenter designing the example used in this chapter might well have conceived of the problem as one that is appropriate for Dunnett's Test. The group in which 6 peers gave the unanimously incorrect answer provides the greatest effect toward conformity. For that reason it could serve as the standard against which all other groups are compared. As noted earlier in this chapter, all remaining groups have some feature that might reduce the effects of conformity The question of interest would be which of these different methods reduces the tendency to conform. The appropriate significance test would be Dunnett's Test with Group I as the control against which all other groups would be compared.

The cost of using Dunnett's Test is that some differences of interest might not be considered. No tests are conducted that compare Groups II through V; rather, they are all compared with the control. Dunnett's Test is advantageous in that it provides a powerful test of significance while controlling Type I error to a reasonable level.

The t-values for Groups II through V compared with Group I as the control groups are as follows:

I compared with II	t = 0.18
I compared with III	t = 4.24
I compared with IV	t = 2.21
I compared with V	t = 2.71

The table provided by Dunnett and found in such texts as Edwards (1985) and Howell (1982) lists the required value of *t* that is based on the number of groups and the number of degrees of freedom on which the MS_{within} was based. With 5 groups including a control group and 120 degrees of freedom, the critical value is 2.47. Of the 4 comparisons, then, two would be significant and two would not.

4. POST HOC COMPARISONS: THE SCHEFFÉ TEST

This chapter describes an important multiple-comparison test that is used to control Type I error in *post hoc* or exploratory experiments—

the Scheffé Test (Scheffé, 1953). As the term implies, post hoc comparisons are developed *after* experimental data have been gathered. The experimenter might notice interesting findings that were not anticipated prior to data collection. Or the researcher might decide to combine all possible aggregations of means to determine which are statistically significant—perhaps to suggest additional experiments that might be run.

Post hoc comparisons account for artificially large amounts of treatment variability. Because the data are examined to find interesting and potentially important relationships, any chance difference that might be present in these data will encourage a post hoc comparison. The difficulty is that the difference expected in a post hoc comparison is not equivalent to the difference expected from a randomly chosen (or predetermined) comparison when Ho is true. Instead, the experimenter must remember that the difference for the post hoc comparison was selected *systematically* because that difference appeared to be large. As a result, the probability of a Type I error will be substantial when Ho is true unless the decision rule for the rejection of Ho will compensate for the expected increase in variability.

To demonstrate this problem, consider a sampling experiment consisting of 4 samples of equal size drawn from a single barrel containing a large set of numbers each written on equivalent pieces of cardboard. Because all samples were drawn from the same barrel, Ho must be true. If the first two samples are combined and compared with the combination of the third and fourth samples, there would be a difference between these two means that reflect only chance differences. If this process were repeated many times, the distribution of differences would vary around zero even though some differences might be large. When the significance tests were conducted, 5% of the differences would be sufficiently large to reject Ho when alpha is set at 5%. This finding holds because the comparisons were determined prior to the collection of data. Compare these results with the expected outcomes if we inspected each sample of 4 means and deliberately combined the two largest means to be compared with the two smallest values. Each difference would capitalize on the effects of chance to produce post hoc comparisons that differed systematically. The significance tests for the post hoc comparisons would result in many more F-ratios exceeding the tabled values for the 5% significance level and therefore rejecting Ho at that level.

CONTROLS FOR REDUCING TYPE I ERRORS IN POST HOC COMPARISONS

The most widely used control for reducing Type I errors in post hoc comparisons was proposed by Scheffé (1953). His procedure permits the testing of any number of post hoc comparisons while maintaining the experimentwise error rate at 5% (or at any other preselected value). This is accomplished by requiring a large value of *F* before the null hypothesis is rejected. The result is a very low per comparison error rate. Scheffé acknowledged that a 5% experimentwise criterion might be too conservative and suggested that the 10% level would be more reasonable. Nonetheless, the 5% level is so widely accepted in other decision rules that any larger criterion is likely to find disfavor with many researchers.

The Scheffé Test is used with post hoc comparisons to provide conservative control over the probability of incorrectly rejecting a Ho. Because it controls Type I error by requiring a particularly large difference between groups before Ho can be rejected, the Scheffé Test is not very powerful. And because its power is low, it cannot be recommended for a small number of planned comparisons.

Scheffé controls the probability of a Type I error by tying the experimentwise error rate to the overall decision concerning the differences between means. The test is so designed that the overall Ho must be rejected before it is possible to reject Ho for a comparison. Because of this, the probability of a Type I error on any comparison within the experiment can be no greater than .05. That is, the Scheffé Test can lead to a rejected Ho for a comparison only in those 5% of the possible experiments in which the overall *F* could reject Ho for the *k* treatment groups.

CONDUCTING THE SCHEFFÉ TEST

The Scheffé Test consists of defining the value of *F* (or *t* if the t-test is preferred) required to limit the experimentwise error rate to 5%. This required value of *F* (called *F'*) is based on the F-value used to reject the overall treatment effects and the number of degrees of freedom found in the treatment sum of squares. The formula for *F'* is:

$$F' = (k-1)(F_{.05}) \qquad (4.1)$$

where k is the number of treatment groups and $F_{.05}$ is the tabled value of F with k–1 degrees of freedom in the numerator and k(n–1) degrees of freedom in the denominator. F is the critical value required to reject the overall Ho. Any F calculated for a particular comparison must surpass F' before it can reject Ho. Using the data obtained from the conformity study (see Chapter 1), the required value of $F' = (k-1)(F_{.05}) = (5-1)(2.44) = 9.76$. Any F-ratio that equals or surpasses 9.76 is significant. The use of the Scheffé Test would be appropriate if the pertinent research were ambiguous regarding those conditions that influence conformity. If the experimental questions warrant the use of the Scheffé Test, the cost is the loss of statistical power that accompanies exploratory analyses.

Table 2 shows that the original F-test resulted in the rejection of Ho. Thus there is sufficient variation among the treatment means to produce a comparison that will also reject Ho. The means for the 5 groups are:

I	II	III	IV	V
5.20	5.08	2.44	3.44	3.76

Various comparisons might be appealing. An obvious question concerns the difference between the combination of Groups I and II (the two largest means) and the remaining 3 groups. Some of the possible comparisons are presented in Table 8. F-ratios that equal or surpass the critical value of 9.76 reject Ho at the 5% level.

Because the Scheffé Test does not restrict the number of comparisons that can be conducted, researchers often compare many more combinations of means than are warranted by their importance. Although an examination of Table 8 shows that many of the comparisons are statistically significant, they also involve one or more of the first two groups with the remaining ones. The comparisons that involved combinations of groups explained the greatest amount of variability. This reflects the increased power derived from larger sample sizes.

CHARACTERISTICS OF THE SCHEFFÉ TEST

Two important and related characteristics of the Scheffé Test are (1) that no null hypothesis for a comparison will be rejected if the overall F-ratio for the treatment effect was insufficient to reject the overall null hypothesis, and (2) that if the original null hypothesis is rejected, there

TABLE 8
Selected Treatment Comparisons Using the Conformity Example Data

Treatments						
I	*II*	*III*	*IV*	*V*	*MS*	*F**
5.20	5.08	2.44	3.44	3.76		
3	3	−2	−2	−2	11.36	21.05
1	1	−1	−1	0	121.00	22.87
1	1	−2	0	0	121.50	22.97
1	1	0	−2	0	48.17	9.11
1	1	0	0	−2	31.74	6.00
1	1	0	−1	−1	59.29	11.21
1	1	−1	0	−1	104.04	19.67
2	0	−1	−1	0	85.13	16.09
2	0	0	−1	−1	42.67	8.07
2	0	−1	0	−1	73.50	13.89
0	2	−1	−1	0	76.33	14.43
0	2	−1	0	−1	65.34	12.35
0	2	0	−1	−1	36.51	6.90
1	0	−1	0	0	95.22	18.00
1	0	0	−1	0	38.72	7.32
1	0	0	0	−1	25.92	4.90
0	1	−1	0	0	87.12	16.47
0	0	2	−1	−1	22.43	4.24
0	0	1	0	−1	21.78	4.12
0	0	1	−1	0	12.50	2.36

*Values of F that equal or surpass 9.76 reject Ho at the .05 significance level.

must be at least one set of weights that will result in a comparison that will reject the null hypothesis.

The preceding two statements are derived from the relationship between the variability associated with a comparison and the variability associated with the treatment sum of squares. A comparison represents an explanation of the variability among means, and the weights provide a model against which the differences in means are compared. If the pattern of the means reflects the pattern in the weights, the comparison will explain or account for a large proportion of the variability in the means. The amount of variability associated with a comparison ranges from zero, when the pattern of weights fails completely to reflect the pattern in the means, to a number equal to the sum of squares for the treatments. This latter value can be obtained only when the pattern of the weights is directly proportional to the pattern in the means. Thus the maximum possible value for the comparison sum of squares is equal to the treatment sum of squares. However, a comparison has one df, while the treatment sum of squares has k–1. When the sum of squares for the comparison and the treatment are divided by their respective degrees of freedom, the mean square for the maximum possible comparison will be k–1 times larger than the treatment sum of squares.

The F-ratio for the maximum possible comparison and the treatment effect both contain the same estimate of random variability in the denominator. Thus the *F* for the maximum possible comparison is greater than the *F* for the overall treatment effect by a factor of k–1. This could happen only when the comparison includes all of the variability in the treatment sum of squares. The critical value that must be surpassed to reject Ho for a comparison using the Scheffé Test is defined as k–1 times the value of *F* that was originally used to evaluate the treatment effect. Hence, if the original value of *F* for the treatment effect did *not* exceed the tabled value, the maximum comparison could not exceed F'.

The second characteristic of the Scheffé Test indicates that if a significant treatment effect is found, at least one comparison exists that will reject the null hypothesis at the same level of significance. Following the previous logic, the maximum possible comparison has an F-ratio that is k–1 times larger than the F-ratio for the treatment effect. If the value of *F* for the treatment is greater than the critical value, the maximum possible *F* for a comparison will be greater that the required value of F'.

The use of the Scheffé Test does not imply that there will always be an interesting or meaningful comparison that will be significant. Rather, the characteristics of that test indicate that there is some linear combination among the means that will produce a significantly large *F* to reject Ho.A comparison defined by the weights 2, 2, –2, –1, –1 would have a sum of squares equal to 128.41 within the total variability of 135.25. This comparison, however, is difficult to justify since it differentially weights the last three treatments. While inappropriate here, differential weighting can be used appropriately, for example, in trend analysis (see Chapter 2). Prior to inspecting the data, it is unlikely that the experimenter would have generated this combination. Thus, if the treatment variability just exceeds the critical value required to produce a significant treatment effect, there might not exist a simple comparison that contains a sufficient portion of the variability to be significant. Rather, the only comparisons that would exceed the critical value of F' would be those that are relatively uninterpretable or meaningless.

By requiring a very large value of F before the null hypothesis can be rejected, the Scheffé Test controls the experimentwise error rate at 5%. The cost, however, is a loss in statistical power. Compare, for example, the decision that would result from the Scheffé Test with the decision that would have resulted if the comparison had been evaluated with a 5% per comparison error rate. In the conformity example the error mean square is based on 120 degrees of freedom, and a 5% per comparison rate would be achieved by finding the 5% level in an F table with 1 and 120 degrees of freedom. This tabled value is 3.92. Thus, if an experimenter were conducting a small number of *planned* comparisons, the Ho would be rejected if the F-value were greater than 3.92. Using the Scheffé procedure, the same comparison is required to produce an F of 9.76 before it can be declared significant. If the experimenter had questioned whether the mean for Group I was statistically different from the average of Groups IV and V, the answer would have been affirmative if that question were asked *before* data were collected; the answer would have been negative if the question came *after* inspecting these means.

Another interesting perspective on the Scheffé Test can be gained by finding the approximate per comparison error rate that corresponds to the critical value of the Scheffé Test. This value can be estimated by using the normal approximation to the t-curve with df > 30. In the current example, the per comparison error rate corresponding to $F' = 9.76$ is approximately .004. Thus the Type I error rate for a comparison is more than 10 times smaller than the .05 level.

The conservative nature of the Scheffé Test is appropriate for the situation for which it was designed. Tight control is needed over Type I errors if there are no a priori hypotheses or if there are so many that every imaginable question is being asked. In these situations the Scheffé Test is used appropriately. However, the Scheffé Test should not be used if only a few planned hypotheses are to be tested; the resultant loss of statistical power argues strongly against doing so. Regardless of the current tendency of many introductory statistics texts to present only one multiple comparison test—usually the Scheffé Test because it will never lead to insufficient control over Type I error—the incorrect use of this test could result in well-planned experiments without sufficient power to reject the null hypothesis when differences between means are due to treatment effects.

One other point needs to be emphasized. Although the Scheffé Test is very conservative regarding experimentwise Type I error, when an error of this type does occur, several comparisons can all capitalize on the same random event, creating serious Type I errors. Thus, although the Scheffé Test is conservative regarding Type I errors, when these errors do occur they can be serious indeed! This difficulty is not so much a reflection of the Scheffé Test itself as it is the experimenter's unwillingness to limit the number of questions asked. If any less conservative criterion were used, the problems of multiple and redundant findings would be greatly intensified.

5. MULTIPLE COMPARISONS IN FACTORIAL DESIGNS

Factorial designs involve two or more independent variables that are analyzed concurrently within an analysis of variance. A completely crossed factorial design consists of all possible pairings of the levels of each of the independent variables.

As an example, consider the experiment on conformity described in Chapter 1. In that example the male participants were tested in the presence of confederates, all of whom were also males. To demonstrate the meaning of a factorial design, we will introduce a second level of sex so that half of the subjects will be tested under condition B_1 (in which all of the confederates are males) and B_2 (in which there are 4 males and 2 females). Group B_2 will involve the placement of a female in the second position within the room. As in the earlier example, 25 males are randomly assigned to each treatment group.

The *A* factor will be reduced to 4 of the original 5 levels to reduce complexity. The treatment that contained only 4 persons will be eliminated. The following conditions of the *A* variable remain:

- A_1 All confederates give the same, incorrect answer on the critical trials
- A_2 The subject in the second position gives the correct answer on the critical trials; the others give the same incorrect answer
- A_3 The confederate in the second position gives an incorrect answer on the critical trials that differs from the incorrect answer given by the other confederate

TABLE 9
Cell Means for a 4 X 2 Factorial Modification of the Conformity Example Data and t-Values for Simple Main Effects

	A_1	A_2	A_3	A_4
B_1	5.20	2.44	3.44	3.76
B_2	4.20	2.08	4.84	5.00
t	1.55	0.50	−2.17	−1.93

TABLE 10
Analysis of Variance Summary Table for a 4 X 2 Factorial Modification of Conformity Example Data

Source of Variation	*SS*	*df*	*MS*	*F*
Between Groups	238.54	7		
A. Type of Group Pressure	180.70	3	60.23	11.63
B. Sex Composition	5.12	1	5.12	<1.00
A X B	52.72	3	17.57	3.39
Within	994.56	192	5.18	

A_4 The confederate in the second position gives an incorrect answer occasionally on noncritical trials; on critical trials this confederate gives the same incorrect answers as do the other confederates

The 4 levels of *A* and the 2 levels of *B* define 8 treatment conditions. The means for these treatments are presented in Table 9 along with the simple main effects to be discussed shortly. The analysis of variance for these data is presented in Table 10. The variability in the treatment means is partitioned into three separate sources: the *A* main effect (degree of group agreement), the *B* main effect (the sex of the confederates), and the interaction between these two main effects. More complex experiments involve a larger number of independent variables as well as interactions.

Three tests of significance are computed: one for each main effect and for the interaction. The questions asked by these three effects are similar to those involved in using orthogonal comparisons except that there may be more than two levels in a factor, which results in the test having more than one degree of freedom. In these instances some method of multiple comparisons must be used to determine which differences among the means are statistically significant. Tests of significance for the main and interaction effects are usually conducted with a 5% per comparison error rate.

FAMILYWISE TYPE I ERROR

When the main effect for an independent variable is significant, there are a number of possible ways to further analyze differences. These methods are identical to those that are available in a one-way experiment. That is, the experimenter might compare all possible pairs of means, conduct planned comparisons, or explore the data for other possible differences. The secondary analyses within the levels of a factor are conducted as if that factor were a separate experiment, and control over Type I error is considered separately for each factor. In those multiple-comparison tests that limit Type I error experimentwise to 5%, this limit would be modified to *5% for all of the comparisons conducted on this factor*. This control over erroneous rejections is called a Type I error *familywise*, where the family reflects the level at which the control is actually maintained. If the experimenter were conducting Dunn's Test, the 5% would be divided among the comparisons present for that main effect and not the number of comparisons conducted within the entire multifactor experiment. The F' value for the Scheffé Test would be based on the tabled value for judging the significance of the main effect and the number of degrees of freedom associated with that effect. Other than the control of Type I error being familywise and the number of treatments being the number of levels within a factor, the multiple-comparison tests proceed as described in the previous chapters.

A NONQUANTITATIVE APPROACH FOR EXAMINING INTERACTIONS

Determining the significance of an interaction is as important as determining the significance of main effects. Nonetheless, the interaction between factors has not been discussed as thoroughly in the literature as have differences among the levels of main effects. When an interaction

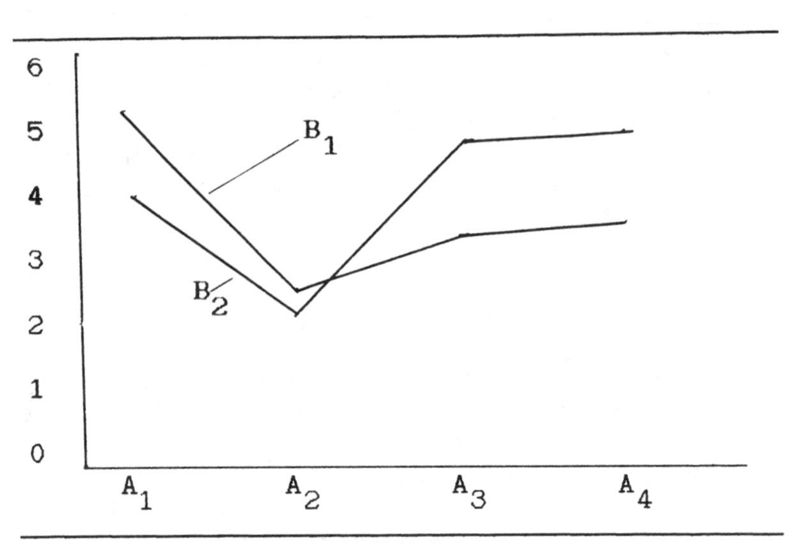

Figure 4: Graph of Means Presented in Table 9

contains more than one df, the location of the difference is uncertain until further analysis is provided. Different procedures are sometimes recommended to identify these interaction effects.

Consider again the cell means in Table 9 and the analysis of variance in Table 10. Each mean in Table 9 was computed on 25 independent subjects. The interaction mean square is given as 17.57 and has 3 degrees of freedom. The within-mean square is 5.18 with 192 dfs, and the overall F-ratio for the interaction effect is 3.39, which exceeds the 5% per comparison tabled value of 2.65.

One widely used procedure to investigate the meaning of the interaction is to graph the relationship between factors. The means in Table 9 are plotted in Figure 4. An examination of this figure indicates that the direction and magnitude of the difference between the male-only group and mixed group differs with A_1 and A_2 producing more conformity within all-male groups, and A_3 and A_4 producing more within mixed groups.

Unfortunately, this description is not an adequate substitute for a test of significance since apparent visual differences can be misleading and manipulated by choice of scale. Researchers are obligated to determine the source of differences between means that enter into interaction effects and attach a probability statement to their decision concerning how likely the finding might be if chance alone were operating.

SIMPLE MAIN EFFECTS

One way to analyze interactions begins with an analysis of *simple main effects*. This approach is particularly convenient when one of the independent variables involved in the interaction has only two levels. A significant interaction is explained by evaluating the differences in one of the independent variables at each level of the other independent variable. In our example simple main effects would follow a significant A×B interaction by examining the differences between one of the factors for all levels of the remaining factor. Because *B* has only two levels, the usual procedure is to examine the differences between B_1 and B_2 for each of the 4 levels of *A*. An alternative would be to investigate the differences between *A* for the two levels of *B*. This approach requires additional analysis to determine where the differences occurred within the 4 means for each level of *B*. Either approach could be appropriate depending on the purpose of the experiment. For the current example, we will concentrate on the differences in *B* for the 4 levels of *A*. Four separate tests of significance will be conducted to determine if the difference between B_1 and B_2, for a specific level of *A*, differs significantly. The intent is to gain a better understanding of the interactions by examining the pattern of significant findings for the four tests of significance.[11]

The simple main effects at each level of *A* are indicated by the t-values in Table 9 listed in the row marked *t for Simple Effects*. Using a 5% per comparison error rate, we would reject the Ho that the means for B_1 and B_2 estimate the same population mean for level A_3. The other three null hypotheses cannot be rejected.

Simple main effects analyze the interaction between variables based on the pattern of significant and nonsignificant differences in the means. The primary limitation of this approach centers on its use of two classes of findings (significant and nonsignificant) rather than direct tests to determine the differences. The result of this division of the differences into these two categories is that we are strongly tempted to overinterpret the meaning of nonsignificant differences and ignore testable differences in the means. The researcher is tempted to explain the meaning of the interaction by concluding that there were differences in the levels of *B* for some of the levels of *A*, and there were no differences for other levels of *A*. This overstates the meaning of a nonsignificant difference to suggest that there were no differences for some levels of *A* rather than that there was insufficient evidence to reject the null hypothesis for some groups. Thus the difference between a significant and a nonsignificant effect is assumed to represent a meaningful basis for differentiating between groups.

A second difficulty is that when several levels of *B* produce significant differences in the *A* effect, there is no procedure for determining whether the magnitude of the two effects is sufficiently different that they should be declared significantly different. Rather, both are presented as producing a significant effect and the difference left untested.

In the present example the simple main effects indicated that the differences between B_1 and B_2 are not significantly different for three of the four comparisons. We are left with the impression that these three levels of *A* produced one effect for *B* (a nonsignificant effect) and that A_3 produced a different effect. By examining the means in Figure 4, however, we find that this grouping does not describe adequately the observed differences in the groups. In particular, the implication that the *B* effect for A_3 and A_4 is different (since one was a significant effect and the other was not) would greatly misrepresent the data. The difference in the *B* effects for these two groups of *A* are more similar than for any other pair of levels of *A*. The problem developed because one comparison barely surpassed the required value of *t* whereas the other was just below the critical value needed to reject Ho. In a later section of this chapter, we will find that the difference between the *B* effect at A_3 and A_4 produces a nonsignificant difference. Such misleading findings are produced by determining the difference indirectly rather than by conducting the comparison between the relevant levels of *A*. If the question regarding the differential effectiveness of *B* at A_3 and A_4 is important, it should be evaluated by a procedure that will permit a probability statement to be made about that difference and not depend on a pattern of significant and nonsignificant findings.

The arguments used against simple main effects would label the decision made on the current data to be a Type IV error. This error is defined as the use of an incorrect multiple comparison on a correctly rejected null hypothesis. Because this topic cannot be resolved here, the interested reader is referred to Games (1973) and Levin and Marascuilo (1972) for a more extensive discussion.

MULTIPLE COMPARISONS ON INTERACTIONS

Another approach for analyzing interactions is to continue to use the same analyses for the interactions as were used in the analysis of the separate independent variables. For example, if the differences between the overall levels of a treatment variable were analyzed using a pairwise method in which all possible pairs of means were compared, a reasonable analysis of the interaction of that variable with other independent variables would be to examine the interaction of each pair of levels with the remaining independent variables. Similarly, if there are a few, planned comparisons of interest, the interaction should investigate how the comparisons act jointly with the other independent variables.

In the current example, variable *B* has only two levels; thus no additional questions can be asked about this main effect. The only question regarding *B* is the difference between groups B_1 and B_2. Variable *A* has 4 levels, and thus more specific questions must be asked to understand where differences in *A* might reside. Throughout this monograph alternatives have been presented for performing this type of analysis depending on the nature of the questions to be answered. Whatever approach can make sense out of the differences in the levels of the *A* main effect is probably equally meaningful with regard to how variable *A* interacts with *B*.

RANGE TESTS AND INTERACTIONS

Assume that an experimenter had analyzed the *A* variable by a pairwise method such as the Newman-Keuls. The questions of interest concern how each mean differs from each of the other means that comprise the 4 levels of *A*. This analysis suggests that the interaction between *A* and *B* might also be analyzed by investigating how each pair of the *A* level arrangements interacts with the two levels of *B*.

The test statistic for range tests is *q*, whereas the interaction comparison is normally expressed as an F-ratio. Either the critical value for *q* must be converted to an F-ratio, or the test statistic must be converted from *F* to *q*. The approach shown here first converts *q* to *t* and then *t* to a comparable value of *F*. The difference between *q* and *t* (see Chapter 2) lies in the standard error used to describe differences between means. The q-statistic uses the standard error of the mean; *t* requires the use of the standard error of the difference between means. The relationship between the two standard errors is given by:

$$S_{\bar{X}_1 - \bar{X}_2} = \sqrt{S^2_{\bar{X}_1} + S^2_{\bar{X}_2}} = S_{\bar{X}}\sqrt{2}$$

To change the critical value from *q* to *t* requires dividing the tabled value of *q* for any of the range tests by the square root of 2. This t-statistic can then be converted to a critical value for *F* since $t^2 = F$.

For the data in Table 10, the within-groups mean square has 192 dfs. Because most tables for the range test do not contain values for all possible degrees of freedom, we have chosen the more conservative approach by entering the table with 120 degrees of freedom. For 120 dfs the tabled values are 3.69 for a range of 4 means, 3.36 for 3 means, and 2.80 for a range of 2 means. After converting the test statistic to F-ratios, the critical values needed to reject Ho using the Newman-Keuls procedure are 6.80 for a range of 4 means, 5.64 for a range of 3 means, and 3.92 for 2 means.

The difference between the mean scores from levels B_2 and B_1 is found for each of the four levels of *A*. These values ($\overline{X}_{B_2} - \overline{X}_{B_1}$) are arranged in ascending order. For the data in Table 10 the values are:

A_1	A_2	A_4	A_3
−1.00	−.36	1.24	1.40

The two levels of *A* that will produce the greatest interaction are those having the greatest difference in effect. These are levels A_1 and A_3. The 2X2 table for this comparison is:

	A_1	A_3
B_1	5.20 (1)	3.44 (−1)
B_2	4.20 (−1)	4.84 (1)

The parenthetical numbers associated with the means are the weights used to find the mean square for the interaction comparison.[12] The value of of *D* for this comparison is:

$$D = (1)(5.20) + (-1)(4.20) + (-1)(3.44) + (1)(4.84)$$

$$D = 2.40$$

The mean square, found by using formula 2.1, is:

$$MS = \frac{25\,(2.4)^2}{4}$$

$$MS = 36.0$$

Dividing this by the MS_W produces an *F* of 6.95. Because these are the two extremes for 4 groups, the interaction would be evaluated against a range of 4. The observed *F* exceeds the converted critical value of 6.80, and Ho is rejected.

The next values to be examined are differences with a range of 3. These are the difference between levels A_1 and A_4 and levels A_2 and A_3. The mean squares for the two comparisons are 31.36 and 19.36, respectively. The F-ratios for the comparisons are 6.05 and 3.74. The *F* for the first comparison exceeds the converted critical value, and Ho is rejected for the range A_1 to A_4 in interaction with *B*. The F-ratio for the interaction of A_2 to A_3 with *B* does not exceed the converted critical value, and that Ho is not rejected. Within the A_1 to A_4 range, there is only one range of 2 groups that is not a part of the nonsignificant range of A_1 and A_2 with *B*. The mean square for the comparison is 2.58 and yields an F-ratio less than 1.0.

The interpretation of these significance tests has been simplified considerably by having only two levels of variable *B*. The test results indicate the the researcher has to consider both sexual composition of the groups and degree of unanimity; neither alone can explain the results adequately. The highest scores are obtained by the A_1B_1 and the A_3B_2 groups. Note also that the mixed-sex group produces less conformity when its members are unanimously opposed to the correct response but less support (and thus greater conformity) if the dissenting member of the group is female. Because the interaction is significant, the main effects must be interpreted cautiously. The type of group pressure has a significant effect on conformity, but the effect is altered by the sexual composition of the group.

Similar procedures could be developed for other pairwise methods. Using Tukey's HSD Test, for example, the converted tabled value for the widest range would be the standard against which all comparisons would be made. Duncan's Test would proceed in the same manner as the Newman-Keuls, with the difference being the converted tabled values. The rationale for conducting these tests has been presented in Chapter 3 of this monograph. As discussed in that chapter, range tests vary in the degree of control they exert over Type I errors, with Tukey's HSD Test being the most conservative and Duncan's Test the most liberal. It is also possible to investigate interaction effects with a modified LSD procedure. The rationale for doing so involves converting the usual t-value to an F-ratio. As described in Chapter 3, the LSD Test would be the most powerful and most likely to commit Type I errors.

PLANNED COMPARISONS AND INTERACTION EFFECTS

If the main effect for *A* had involved a small number of planned comparisons, the interaction should also investigate the way in which these comparisons interact with the other independent variable. The task is again simplified by having only two groups in variable *B*. These two levels can be assigned weights of +1 and −1. The following questions of interest regarding the *A* effect are derived from the discussion of this topic in Chapter 2.

The first comparison involves the average of all groups in which there was some break in the unanimity of responses. For the current example with only 4 levels of the *A* factor, the weights are 3, −1, −1, −1. The second comparison of interest for this factor is the difference between the group in which the subject had one other person responding correctly and the two groups in which an individual differed from the majority but failed to support the correct response. The weights for this comparison are 0, 2, −1, −1. The third comparison in this set involves the difference between the two groups that gave deviant and incorrect responses. Group 3 confederates gave deviant and incorrect responses on the critical trials; the Group 4 confederates, in contrast, gave deviant responses only on the noncritical trials (that is, those trials in which all other confederates gave the correct response). The weights for this comparison are 0, 0, 1, −1. These three comparisons are orthogonal and provide a complete partition of the variability in factor *A*.

The analysis of the interaction with planned comparisons involves the generation of a set of weights to apply to the cell means of the interaction table. These weights are found by multiplying the weights for the 2 main effects. Table 11a presents the weights to be applied to the treatment means for the interaction of the first comparison and the *B* factor. Each cell weight is the product of the weight for the row and column that define that cell. The weights for the interaction of the remaining two comparisons on the *A* effect and *B* are contained in Table 11b and c.

The mean square for each comparison is calculated as before using formula 2.1. These mean squares are divided by the within-groups MS to produce an F-ratio. The within-groups MS for this example was given in Table 10 as 5.18; thus the F-ratios are as follows:

$$F_1 = 29.04/5.18 = 5.61$$
$$F_2 = 23.52/5.18 = 4.54$$
$$F_3 = .16/5.18 = < 1$$

TABLE 11
Weights for Planned Comparisons on Interaction

a

		A_1	A_2	A_3	A_4
		3	−1	−1	−1
B_1	1	3	−1	−1	−1
B_2	−1	−3	1	1	1

b

		A_1	A_2	A_3	A_4
		0	2	−1	−1
B_1	1	0	2	−1	−1
B_2	−1	0	−2	1	1

c

		A_1	A_2	A_3	A_4
		0	0	1	−1
B_1	1	0	0	1	−1
B_2	−1	0	0	−1	1

Whether Ho will be rejected or not depends on the decision rule that is adopted. The two most commonly used decision rules are that a 5% per comparison error rate will be adopted or that Dunn's recommendation to divide the 5% among the three comparisons will be followed. Using the 5% per comparison decision rule, both F_1 and F_2 are large enough to result in the null hypothesis being rejected. The F-ratio for the interaction of the third comparison with the levels of factor *B* is not significant. If the more conservative decision rule proposed by Dunn were used, none of the three interactions would be significant. This would leave the experimenter with an unanswered question regarding the interaction effect.

Following the same logic, Scheffé's Test can be modified to analyze the data in Table 9. Each of the two independent variables can be analyzed into whatever comparisons are of interest. The weights for each comparison are found by multiplying the weights for each of the factors. The mean square is calculated in the same manner as with planned comparisons and an F-ratio found by dividing by the within-groups MS. The critical value for evaluating *F* is the product of the original critical *F* for the interaction and the appropriate number of degrees of freedom for that interaction. As is true for the Scheffé Test for the main effects, no comparisons will result in a rejection of Ho if the overall interaction could not reject Ho. This procedure is conservative and is especially so as the number of degrees of freedom for the interaction increases.

6. ADDITIONAL CONSIDERATIONS

UNEQUAL SAMPLE SIZES

Most experimental designs assign an equal number of subjects to each treatment group to provide maximum power for a specific number of total subjects. Unfortunately, "experimental mortality," the difficulty in locating experimental subjects, and the difficulty in using subjects more than once, all combine to reduce the sample size and statistical power. When differences in sample sizes are relatively small and can be attributed to random factors, the methods presented in this monograph can be used with minor modifications. When differences in sample sizes are large, the use of the methods presented becomes more problematic. Of particular concern is the confounding of effects with unequal sample sizes.

PAIRWISE COMPARISONS

Chapter 2 on *Pairwise Comparisons* described the use of the range statistic, *q*, and the t-statistic. The t-tests do not require equal *n*s, and thus no elaboration is needed here. The use of range tests, however, raises two problems when the *n*s are not equal. The first problem is to determine the appropriate value to substitute for *n* in the formula for the standard error of the mean; the second problem is related to the specific nature of the decision rules when sequential tests of significance (such as Newman-Keuls or the Duncan Tests) are used. The q-statistic is expressed as the number of standard errors of the mean that exist between the two extreme means being compared. The use of *q* assumes equal numbers of subjects in each sample, so that when Ho is true, all sample means within the set are drawn from the same sampling distribution. With different numbers of subjects, each sample mean is, in effect, drawn from a different sampling distribution. This lack of congruence between the data and the model has lead to several suggestions for modifying these procedures.

When differences in sample sizes are relatively small, the most common solution for unequal *n*s is to substitute the *harmonic mean* of the sample sizes for the *n* in the formula for the standard error of the mean. The harmonic mean (rather than the arithmetic mean) is used to estimate the average effect of division by different values of *n*. The formula for the harmonic mean ($\bar{n}_h$) is:

$$\bar{n}_h = \frac{k}{1/n_1 + 1/n_2 + \ldots + 1/n_k} \qquad (5.2)$$

where *k* is the number of treatment groups. The standard error of the mean (using the harmonic mean's estimated sample size) is used to measure the distance between the means as if the *n*s were equal.

When there are larger differences in sample sizes, the harmonic mean of *n* for the two groups being compared is used in the formula for the standard error of the mean (Kramer, 1956). The average *n* will differ for each comparison since only the *n*s of the pair of means will be used. Although this procedure requires more effort, it is also more responsive to differences in *n*. Another possibility is to use the smallest sample size for *n* (Spotvoll and Stoline, 1973) to provide a conservative statistical test.

Assuming homogeneity of variance and small differences[13] in the values of *n*, our recommendation is to use the harmonic mean of all sample sizes. As these differences increase, the preferred procedure is to use only those samples being compared, as Kramer (1956) suggested.

Another concern with unequal *n*s is the reasonableness of sequential significance tests (e.g., Duncan and Newman-Keuls Tests). The significance of the difference between two means depends on the sizes of the relevant samples. A difference based on small sample sizes could easily result in the failure to reject Ho, while a similar or even smaller difference could reject Ho if sample sizes were larger. The relationship between *n* and *q* can lead to a nonrejected Ho if the two extreme means are based on small sample sizes when the standard error is computed by using their respective *n*s. At the same time, a difference between interior means based on much larger *n*s could represent an important and significant difference *if* tested. With either the Newman-Keuls or Duncan's Test, the interior ranges would not be tested for significance if the wider range were not significant. Thus a sequential test could result in an unacceptable restriction concerning those differences that require testing.

The degree of unacceptability may be reduced by testing the interior ranges that are based on larger *n*s even if the wider range were not significant. Another suggestion is to use the harmonic mean of all samples within the experiment rather than only the sample sizes of the groups being compared. A third "solution" is to abandon the sequential tests in favor of one that maintains a constant value of *q* regardless of range. The first two "solutions" described in this paragraph could result in inflated Type I error rates and are unacceptable. The third solution creates tests that are slightly more conservative with respect to Type I error, but this seems preferable to inflating the error rate. Thus our recommendation is to use Tukey's HSD rather than the Newman-Keuls. Those favoring more liberal control over Type I error with the associated increase in power might use a lower critical value, such as the widest range from Duncan's table for all comparisons.

A PRIORI COMPARISONS

Two procedures involving a priori comparisons may be used with unequal *n*s. These procedures are to (1) *weight* each mean by the number of observations on which it was computed or to (2) *unweight* each mean as if it were computed on an equal number of subjects.

If the sample sizes are similar, the value of *n* in the formula for a comparison mean square can be replaced by the harmonic mean of the sample sizes. This procedure is the *unweighted means* approach. Each comparison will analyze the data as if they were derived from an experiment in which each group contained the harmonic mean number of subjects. If orthogonal comparisons are conducted, the unweighted means approach will retain the orthogonality of these comparisons. The sum of a set of orthogonal comparisons will only equal the treatment sum of squares after it is recalculated with groups based on the harmonic mean number of subjects.

The *weighted means* approach is computed by using the actual number of subjects found within the groups. If comparisons involve combinations of groups, each group in the combination will be based on its unique sample size. Should the number of subjects be similar within the treatment groups, the difference between the two approaches will be small and of little consequence. A large difference in the sample sizes, however, can lead to radically different conclusions.

As an example of the possible effects of using weighted or unweighted means, consider a three-group experiment in which the means are 10.0, 13.0, and 14.0. Further, let the sample sizes for the three groups be 20, 5, and 10, respectively. If the comparison of primary interest is the difference between the average of groups 1 and 2 versus group 3, that comparison would be between an average of 14 for group 3 and either an unweighted mean of $(10+13)/2 = 11.5$ for groups 1 and 2 or a weighted mean of $(20)(10)+(5)(13)/(20+5) = 265/25 = 10.6$. A difference of this magnitude (i.e., $11.5–10.6 = 0.9$) could easily influence the significance test.

Which of these two approaches should be used depends, in part, on the researcher's belief about the underlying reason for the differences in *ns*. If a difference reflects the existence of the groups within a population, then the unweighted approach is defensible since it more closely reflects the parameter value. If, however, the difference is due to other considerations (e.g., treatment 2 might be very expensive to conduct, making it feasible to use only 5 subjects), then a weighted means approach would be defensible. Neither approach represents the ideal for evaluating randomly assigned treatments in which equal *ns* would have been preferred.

The Scheffé Test represents a series of comparisons and conceivably could be approached using either weighted or unweighted means. If the 5% Type I error rate experimentwise is to hold exactly, weighted means should be used since the critical value is based on the original *F* used to evaluate the treatment effects. Because the treatment sum of squares takes into effect the number of subjects contained within groups, the critical value of *F* with the Scheffé Test will reflect differences in sample sizes.

VIOLATIONS OF ASSUMPTIONS

F, *t*, and *q* statistics assume that (1) the variances within treatment groups estimate a common population variance, and that (2) the samples are drawn from normal distributions. A considerable body of literature has investigated the effects on Type I error and on statistical power as the consequence of violating these assumptions (see Glass, Sanders, and Peckham, 1972).

Of the five methods for conducting pairwise comparisons discussed in Chapter 3, recent literature has been devoted to adapting Tukey's HSD and the LSD Tests for use with heterogeneous variances and unequal sample sizes. Keselman and Rogan (1978) and Keselman, Games, and Rogan (1979*a*) compared various modifications of Tukey's HSD to control the probability of a Type I error when variances were heterogeneous. These modifications varied the numerical values for *n* used in the formula for the standard error and either assumed a pooled variance estimate or used separate variance estimates from each sample. They concluded that the best control over Type I error was maintained by using a procedure proposed by Games and Howell (1976) tailored after an earlier solution to the Behrens-Fisher problem by Welch (1947).

The Behrens-Fisher problem is the name given to testing differences in means when both variances and sample sizes are unequal. Various solutions have been proposed to maintain the Type I error rate at 5%. The Games and Howell solution involves two parts: first, the difference between the means is divided by a standard error that uses separate rather than a pooled variance estimate. That standard error is defined by:

$$S_{\bar{x}_1-\bar{x}_2} = \sqrt{\frac{S_1^2}{n_1} + \frac{S_2^2}{n_2}} \tag{5.3}$$

Second, the computed value of *t* is evaluated against the tabled value using a reduced number of degrees of freedom. The appropriate number of degrees of freedom has been a topic of continuing controversy. The formula used by Games and Howell is:

$$df' = \frac{\left(\frac{S_1^2}{n_1} + \frac{S_2^2}{n_2}\right)^2}{\frac{\left(\frac{S_1^2}{n_1}\right)^2}{n_1 - 1} + \frac{\left(\frac{S_2^2}{n_2}\right)^2}{n_2 - 1}} \tag{5.4}$$

When Tukey's HSD was modified by these two formulas, the experimentwise Type I error rates were acceptably close to the 5% stated level regardless of heterogeneity of variance or differences in sample size. However, these modifications require a different standard error for each pair of means and a corresponding value for df′. To avoid some of these complexities, Howell (1982) has suggested that experimenters use the tabled values for the smallest possible number of degrees of freedom, which is n–1 where *n* is the smallest sample size. If the tabled value for this minimum number of degrees of freedom is smaller than the observed values of *t*, the researcher can be confident that the observed *t* will be larger than the tabled values if df′ were used. The exact value of df′ would need to be calculated only if the observed value was slightly smaller than the tabled values using the minimum number of degrees of freedom.

The Least Significant Difference Test has also been investigated to determine the effects of heterogeneous variances and unequal sample sizes. Procedurally, the experimenter conducts the omnibus test of significance to determine if differences among treatments are significant. Multiple-comparison tests are used only if the original Ho can be rejected. Unequal sample sizes and heterogeneous variances affect both the probability of a Type I error for the omnibus test and the later LSD comparisons. Keselman, Games, and Rogan (1979*b*) investigated these effects on the omnibus test and on modifications of the LSD Test. They reported large Type I error rates when group variance was related inversely to sample size. They also found that modifications of the omnibus test and the LSD procedures that best controlled the Type I error rate to 5% had been proposed earlier by Welch (1947, 1951). The omnibus test was modified by weighting the treatment means to reflect both sample size and group variance (Welch, 1951); the LSD procedure was modified (as described previously) by using separate variance estimates and a reduced number of degrees of freedom.

With the Scheffé Test, control over Type I error depends on the original test of significance. If the error rate for the omnibus test differs from 5%, the Scheffé experimentwise error rate will also differ from 5%. If the smaller variances are associated with larger samples, the within variance will be underestimated, and the probability of a Type I error will surpass 5%. The modification suggested by Welch (1951) for the omnibus test could be used to compute Scheffé's F', especially if variances and sample sizes differ.

Sequential procedures such as the Newman-Keuls or Duncan's Test are not recommended if there are unequal *n*s or heterogeneous variances. A sequential test could result in the failure to conduct meaningful and otherwise justifiable tests of significance because the wider range could not be rejected.

The one procedure that is most justifiable when there are heterogeneous variances is Tukey's HSD as modified by Games and Howell (1976). The modification does not require that wider ranges be significant before interior ranges are tested. The HSD is conservative in controlling the Type I error rate at 5% experimentwise for all null hypotheses. The LSD Test is not recommended because it controls Type I error experimentwise to 5%, but only for the omnibus test. It does not adequately control false rejections of the partial null hypothesis. The modifications needed for the LSD omnibus test with heterogeneous variances and unequal sample sizes are also more complex and time consuming than are those for the HSD.

Welch's (1947) solution for resolving the Behrens-Fisher problem involves working directly with *a priori* comparisons and heterogeneous variances. The groups being compared would be evaluated by using separate variance estimates and separate sample sizes. The observed value of t or F would be compared with the tabled value using a reduced number of degrees of freedom. The number of degrees of freedom depends on the differences in the variances. The problem is made more difficult if the comparison involves sets of combined groups (e.g., groups 1 and 2 compared with groups 3 and 4). If all groups have heterogeneous variances, it is unclear what the variance estimates would be if Welch's method were used. A compromise in this situation is to use the average variance and a reduced number of degrees of freedom for the tabled values of t or F. A conservative test would use the number of degrees of freedom for the smallest sample. A conservative test is particularly important if the largest sample sizes are paired with the smallest variances. In this case the measure of random variability will be underestimated.

CONCLUDING REMARKS

Throughout this monograph we have adopted the practice of using a simple randomized group design to provide examples of multiple-comparison techniques. These methods can be modified easily for use with more complex designs such as randomized blocks, split plots, or

Latin Squares (see Jaccard, Beckev, and Wood, 1984). The modifications involve finding the appropriate measure of random variability to use in the computation of the *F*, *t*, or *q* statistic. Usually the correct mean square for conducting multiple comparisons is the mean square used for the omnibus test of the treatment effect. Some exceptions, such as repeated measures designs and those involving a quasi-F-test, require more complex measures of random variability that cannot be described adequately in an introductory exposition.

The methods presented in this monograph are those that are most commonly found in the social and behavioral sciences. The research literature is beginning to include some nonparametric procedures for testing multiple comparisons and methods for conducting these comparisons with nonparametric data. Additionally, methods are available that address such problems as determining the *best* of several treatments. Extensive work is also being conducted on the effects of violating assumptions that underlie multiple-comparison tests.

Our orientation in this paper has been within the traditions of the social and behavioral sciences in emphasizing tests of significance. A more mathematically oriented presentation would have described the same topics as discussed here but with greater reliance on the use of confidence intervals instead of significance tests.

In addition to determining whether an effect is significant or not, an additional concern that has received considerable attention is that of *effect size*. This topic involves determining the amount of variance accounted for by a comparison. Unfortunately, like so many other intriguing problems, that topic goes beyond the scope of this paper. Nonetheless, the study of multiple comparisons is not only necessary in its own right, but it also provides a basic understanding required for more advanced study. Thus this monograph should be considered as an *introduction* to new information and not as a conclusion to learning about multiple-comparison tests.

NOTES

1. For those unfamiliar with ANOVA, additional readings in an elementary statistics book such as Howell (1982) or Ferguson (1981) may make this monograph easier to understand. For most readers, however, this brief review should suffice. The role of analysis of variance in multiple comparisons depends on the particular method. Some of those presented will require that the ANOVA be conducted and result in a significant difference. Other procedures contain an omnibus test of significance that replaces the need for an analysis of variance. Even though all methods of multiple comparisons do not require an analysis of variance, this review is included as an introduction to the logic of hypothesis testing and to introduce the vocabulary needed throughout the monograph.

2. The F-ratio was named by Snedecor to honor R. A. Fisher who did much of the pioneering work on the analysis of variance.

3. More specifically, the *power* of a statistical test is defined as the probability of rejecting a false null hypothesis. The analysis of variance is a powerful statistical method since it is highly sensitive to and reflective of differences among multiple means. If β is the probability of committing a Type II error when there are "real" differences among population means, power is $1-\beta$.

4. Although we will explain the rationale behind this approach in Chapter 2, at this point it is necessary to point out that the weights of +1 and −1 are used for simplicity. Any other two values could have been chosen as long as the weights sum to zero. If two means are compared, one weight will be positive and the other negative. Two zeroes are assigned to two group means that are *not* being compared.

5. The above discussion assumes equal sample sizes for the treatment groups. The concept of orthogonality with unequal sample sizes is more complex and will be discussed in Chapter 6.

6. The weights can also be found by cross-multiplying the weights for the first two comparisons. Comparisons involving interactions will be discussed in Chapter 5.

7. Orthogonal comparisons are independent, not mutually exclusive. It is possible, though relatively unlikely, that more than one Type I error could occur in an experiment. In the conformity experiment the experimentwise Type I error rate for the 4 independent comparisons is .19. This is slightly less than the sum of the per comparison error rates of .20.

8. The experimentwise error rate was estimated by interpolating between known probability for tabled values of q.

9. The t-values are converted to corresponding values of q by multiplying the value of t by the square root of 2.

10. As before, these probabilities are obtained by interpolation.

11. The information contained in the four simple main effects consists of the sum of squares previously contained in the A×B interaction and the B main effect.

12. As mentioned in Chapter 2, the weights for the interaction effect in a 2×2 design consist of combining diagonals and can be found by cross-multiplying the weights for the two separate main effects.

13. Ferguson (1981) reports a chi-square test to determine if the observed sample sizes differ sufficiently to represent a significant difference.

REFERENCES

ALLEN, V. L. (1965) "Situational Factors in Conformity," in L. Berkowitz (ed.), Advances in Experimental Social Psychology, Vol. 2. New York: Academic Press.

ASCH, S. E. (1951) "Effects of Group Pressure Upon the Modification and Distortion of Judgment," in H. Guetzkow (ed.), Groups, Leadership, and Men. Pittsburgh, PA: Carnegie Press.

ASCH, S. E. (1952) Social Psychology. Englewood Cliffs, NJ: Prentice-Hall.

ASCH, S. E. (1956) "Studies of Independence and Submission to Group Pressure: I. A Minority of One Against a Unanimous Majority." Psychological Monographs 70: 9 (Whole No. 417).

CRUTCHFIELD, R. S. (1959) "Personal and Situational Factors in Conformity to Group Pressure." Acta Psychologica. 15: 386-388.

DUNCAN, D. B. (1955) "Multiple Range and Multiple F Tests." Biometrics 11: 1-42.

DUNN, O. J. (1961) "Multiple Comparisons Among Means." J. of the American Statistical Assn. 56: 52-64.

DUNNETT, C. W. (1955) "A Multiple Comparison Procedure for Comparing Several Treatments with a Control." J. of the American Statistical Assn. 50: 1096-1121.

EDWARDS, A. L. (1984) An Introduction to Linear Regression and Correlation, 2nd Ed. New York: Freeman.

EDWARDS, A. L. (1985) Experimental Design in Psychological Research, 5th Ed. New York: Harper & Row.

FERGUSON, G. A. (1981) Statistical Analysis in Psychology and Education, 5th Ed. New York: McGraw-Hill.

GAMES, P. A. (1973) "Type IV Errors Revisited." Psychological Bulletin 80: 304-307.

GAMES, P. A. and J. F. HOWELL (1976) "Pairwise Multiple Comparison Procedures with Unequal N's and/or Variances: A Monte Carlo Study." J. of Educational Statistics 1: 113-125.

GERARD, H. B., R. A. WILHELMY, and E. S. CONNOLLEY (1968) "Conformity and Group Size." J. of Personality and Social Psychology 8: 79-82.

GLASS, G. V, J. R. SANDERS, and P. D. PECKHAM (1972) "Consequences of Failure to Meet Assumptions Underlying the Fixed Effects Analysis of Variance and Covariance." Review of Educational Research 42: 237-288.

HOWELL, D. C. (1982) Statistical Methods for Psychology. Boston: Duxbury.

JACCARD, J., M. A. BECKER, and G. WOOD (1984) "Pairwise Multiple Comparison Procedures: A Review." Psychological Bulletin 96: 589-596.

KEPPEL, G. (1982) Design and Analysis: A Researcher's Handbook, 2nd Ed. Englewood Cliffs, NJ: Prentice-Hall.

KESELMAN, H. J. and J. C. ROGAN (1978) "A Comparison of the Modified-Tukey and Scheffé Methods of Multiple Comparisons for Pairwise Contrasts." J. of the American Statistical Assn. 73: 47-52.

KESELMAN, H. J., P. A. GAMES, and J. C. ROGAN (1979*a*) "An Addendum to A Comparison of the Modified-Tukey and Scheffé Methods of Multiple Comparisons for Pairwise Contrasts." J. of the American Statistical Assn. 74: 626-627.

KESELMAN, H. J., P. A. GAMES, and J. C. ROGAN (1979*b*) "Protecting the Overall Rate of Type I Errors for Pairwise Comparisons with an Omnibus Test Statistic." Psychological Bulletin 86: 884-888.

KEULS, M. (1952) "The Use of the Studentized Range in Connection with the Analysis of Variance." Euphytica 1: 112-122.

KRAMER, C. Y. (1956) "Extension of Multiple Range Tests to Group Means with Unequal Numbers of Replications." Biometrics 12: 307-310.

LEVIN, J. R. and L. A. MARASCUILO (1972) "Type IV Errors and Interactions." Psychological Bulletin 78: 368-374.

NEWMAN, D. (1939) "The Distribution of the Range in Samples from a Normal Population in Terms of an Independent Estimate of the Standard Deviation." Biometrika 31: 20-30.

SCHEFFÉ, H. (1953) "A Method for Judging All Contrasts in the Analysis of Variance." Biometrika 40: 87-104.

SPOTVOLL, E. and M. R. STOLINE (1973) "An Extension of the T-Method of Multiple Comparisons to Include the Cases with Unequal Sample Sizes." J. of the American Statistical Assn. 69: 975-978.

TUKEY, J. W. (1953) "The Problem of Multiple Comparisons." Unpublished manuscript.

WELCH, B. L. (1947) "The Generalization of Student's Problem when Several Different Population Variances are Involved." Biometrika 34: 28-35.

WELCH, B. L. (1951) "On the Comparison of Several Mean Values: An Alternative Approach." Biometrika 38: 330-336.

ALAN J. KLOCKARS *is Professor of Educational Psychology at the University of Washington. He received his undergraduate and master's degrees at Oregon State University and his doctorate in Psychology from the University of Washington. He has published on the methodological and measurement issues in journals such as* Applied Psychological Measurements, Educational and Psychological Measurement, Journal of Educational Measurement, *and* Journal of Research on Alcohol. *He is currently involved in research on rating scales and affective measurement.*

GILBERT SAX *is Professor of Education and Psychology at the University of Washington where he is conducting research on test construction and evaluation. He is author of two college-level texts that are used in courses on research methods and on educational and psychological measurement. He has served on the editorial review boards of various journals and has been the principal investigator on numerous research and evaluation studies. He received his Ph.D. in Educational Psychology from the University of Southern California.*